KINGS OF THE RINK

KINGS OF THE RINK

Stan Fischler

ILLUSTRATED WITH PHOTOGRAPHS

DODD, MEAD & COMPANY · New York

PICTURE CREDITS
Jim Anderson: 21, 23, 41, 43, 46, 52, 67, 73, 76, 79, 82, 88, 91, 93, 96, 99. Steve Namm: 15, 26, 35, 58, 70, 81. UPI: 4, 12, 17, 19, 24, 29, 31, 32, 36, 38, 50, 55, 60, 62, 64, 85, 95, 100.

Frontispiece: The puck sails over a kneeling Ken Dryden.

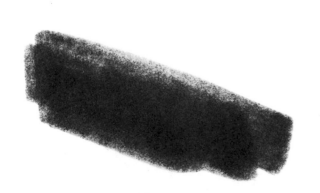

1 2 3 4 5 6 7 8 9 10

Library of Congress Cataloging in Publication Data

Fischler, Stan.

  Kings of the rink.
  Includes index.
  SUMMARY: Discusses the hockey careers of Syl Apps
II, Bobby Clarke, Marcel Dionne, Ken Dryden, Guy Lafleur,
Brad Park, Denis Potvin, and Darryl Sittler.
  1. Hockey players—Juvenile literature. [1. Hockey
players] I. Title.
GV847.25.F55   796.9′62′0922 [B] [920]   78-7727
ISBN 0–396–07609–2

CONTENTS

INTRODUCTION

It all started in 1937.

My love affair with hockey, that is. Who would have believed it at the time? I was enroute to see *Snow White and the Seven Dwarfs* with my father but we were detoured at Madison Square Garden. A mere five-year-old, I knew nothing of stick, puck or playoffs. But I knew much about Sleepy, Dopey, Grumpy and the rest. And, of course, I was infatuated with Snow White.

That's why I was furious with Dad when he informed me that, no, we weren't going to see the film. It was raining in torrents when we emerged from the subway station and the theater was a good six blocks away. No umbrella, no Snow White. "I am going to take you to see a hockey game," said my father.

His logic was impeccable. Madison Square Garden was a mere ten yards from the rain-drenched subway station. The hockey game cost only 50 cents and he loved hockey.

I sat down and cried.

Whenever five-year-old Stanley burst into tears, father Fischler did the opposite from what his son whimpered. Thus, we marched into the Garden to see the New York Rovers play the Washington Eagles. From that point, Stan Fischler was hooked on hockey for life.

Like all love affairs it has had its ups and downs. Let's forget about the downers. The ups, among others, have been grand moments watching Hall of Famers such as Maurice "Rocket" Richard careen around an enemy defenseman and score another goal for the Montreal Canadiens. Or delighting in the dipsy-doodle dandy of Delisle, Saskatchewan—Max Bentley of the Maple Leafs. Or sitting awestruck as Ranger Goalie Chuck Rayner extended his bulky, leather pads from here to there to punt out a screened shot to the far corner.

For a 45-year-old, it is easy to lapse into the nostalgia of a National Hockey League that boasted only six teams. That's the way things were when I was a growing fan; and that's the way things were until expansion took place in 1967. Oldtimers are quick to criticize the contemporary game. Sure, it "ain't what it used to be" but neither is the old gray mare.

Since the advent of expansion, a new breed of classy and crafty artists has developed. It is fashionable for the Old Guard to say there never has been a digger like Ted "Teeder" Kennedy, captain of the

Stanley Cup-winning Toronto Maple Leafs in 1949. True, Teeder was a gem, but nobody works harder, or is a greater inspiration than Philadelphia Flyers' Captain Bobby Clarke. Likewise, nostalgics enjoy telling young fans about the goaltending exploits of the late Terry Sawchuk. No one could quibble with that. But when has there ever been a more fascinating—he is a lawyer—or accomplished goaltender than Ken Dryden, who always seems to be leading the Canadiens to another Stanley Cup?

Hockey was a grand game in 1937, a perfect delight in 1947, a challenge to write about in 1957, a fascinating growth industry when it expanded in 1967 and just as much fun as ever in 1978. If I'm lucky, my love affair with stick and puck will continue on to 1988 and one of the reasons will be the artists described here.

With all deference to the Seven Dwarfs, I'm glad we didn't go to see *Snow White* on that rainy day in 1937.

Stan Fischler

KINGS OF THE RINK

Syl Apps versus Chicago's Keith Magnuson

SYL APPS II

Syl Apps II had a tough act to follow. His father, Syl I, starred twelve years for the Toronto Maple Leafs, scoring 201 goals in an era when a 200-goal career total was something extraordinary. The elder Apps, a member of hockey's Hall of Fame, led the Maple Leafs to Stanley Cup victories in 1942, and two straight in 1947 and 1948. Naturally, once Syl II started playing, he heard all the comparisons—with the verdict that young Apps never could be as good as his father. Ultimately, such talk had to have a psychological impact.

"I used to feel pressures when I was growing up," Syl recalls. "From kids' hockey in Canada right through my upper Junior days, the fans would say the only reason I was playing was because of my father's name. But I soon learned that you reach a point where, if you're not good enough, a name isn't going to win you a job. You have to do it on your own ability."

As a youngster, Syl never dreamed of being a big-league hockey star; he remained at home in Kingston, Ontario, and concentrated on his schoolwork.

"My father never pushed me in hockey," he says. "The only thing he kept pushing me about was school. He always threatened to make me quit hockey if my marks slipped below 70. But I never did find out if he ever really meant it."

After graduating from midget hockey ranks, Syl played for the Kingston Frontenacs Seniors Club. His improvement was suitably steady and it surprised some observers that the Toronto Maple Leafs were not interested in the son of one of the greatest stars in their history. But young Syl had an analysis of the situation.

"I can't say I was puzzled that the Leafs showed no interest in me," he explains. "To begin with, I never played any Junior A hockey. I knew that the fast Junior A league is where they look for their players. Besides, I never had set my sights on being a professional athlete. From the day I graduated high school, the idea always was that I would continue on to college. And that's exactly what I did!"

Even though the New York Rangers drafted Syl on the fourth round in 1964 and were waiting with a lucrative contract, Apps said "thanks-but-no-thanks" and left for Princeton University. Johnny Wilson, who has since coached several professional teams as well as Team Canada 1977 in the World Championship tournament in Vienna, was coaching Princeton at the time.

"Educationally, Princeton was great," Syl remembers, "but financially it was too expensive. They didn't grant a scholarship. Whatever aid I got was based on what they decided I needed. They decided I needed $500. It cost me $5500. Anyhow, I played freshman hockey, and didn't have an especially good year. The players weren't strong and I found it more difficult to look good with bad players than with good ones. The bad ones tended to get in my way."

Syl reluctantly quit Princeton and returned home. He enrolled at Queen's College and also signed with the speedy Kingston Aces of the Ontario Hockey Association Senior Division. He regained his good form and, at the age of 22, finally changed his mind about playing pro hockey. "All of a sudden," he says, "I realized I had a chance at the NHL, so I went to work getting to the top. My father told me to give it three good years. If I didn't make it by then, I could quit and go into something else. I figured I didn't have much to lose. What's the difference if you get started in the business world when you're twenty-two or twenty-five?"

With that in mind, Syl attended the Rangers' camp in the fall of 1969, and signed a two-year contract with the New York club. He impressed the scouts and was assigned to the Rangers' farm team in Omaha of the Central Hockey League. The Rangers' scouting report on Apps read: "steady, but unspectacular."

At Omaha, Syl had a modest 1969-70 season, scoring 16 goals and 38 assists for 54 points in 68 games. But in the playoffs, he exploded for 10 goals and 9 assists for 19 points in only 12 games, leading Omaha to the Central League championship. The Rangers rewarded him with a promotion to Buffalo of the American Hockey League farm club for the playoffs. Although he found himself on a new team, Syl responded with two goals and three assists in seven American League playoff games.

Now, the scouting report was embellished: "Apps is a splendid skater, a good puck-handler and playmaker, just like his father."

The next step was the National Hockey League, and, indeed, on opening night of the 1970–71 season, Sylvanus Marshall Apps II was wearing a New York Rangers uniform. He launched his NHL career on a line with Vic Hadfield and Bob Nevin, but the bubble quickly burst and he soon found himself on the bench.

"I made too many mistakes," he admits. "Maybe I was trying too hard. When the Rangers made a deal to get Pete Stemkowski (on October 31), I knew I wasn't going to get much action. I picked up a lot of splinters."

Stemkowski, along with Walt Tkaczuk and Jean Ratelle, provided the New Yorkers with three solid, experienced veteran centers, so Apps sat and sat. He managed only one goal and two assists in parts of 31 games before being dispatched to Omaha. Syl was stunned but resigned.

"At the time," he explains, "the Rangers were fighting for first place, and they didn't have much confidence in me. In that kind of situation even one goal could make a difference, and it was tough for them to use an inexperienced man like me."

Discouraged, he returned to Omaha, where he scored no goals and five assists in eleven games before getting his big break. It was a case of "sweet are the uses of adversity." On January 26, 1971, the Rangers traded Syl to the Pittsburgh Penguins for Glen Sather, a penalty-killer sought by Ranger General Manager Emile Francis for years.

Once again, Syl found himself in an uncomfortable spot. The colorful Sather had been a popular player in Pittsburgh, and Penguins fans were suitably incensed over the deal. When Syl skated onto the ice for the first time in a Pittsburgh uniform, he was greeted by a large banner reading: WHY SLATS?

Ironically, Syl's first game was against his father's former team: the Maple Leafs. The latter-day Apps gave the Leafs—and the rest of the NHL—a preview of things to come as he marked his Pittsburgh debut with a goal and an assist. His new coach, Red Kelly, remembers Syl's first goal as a Penguin:

"Jacques Plante was in the Toronto nets. Syl skated in alone, one-on-one, against Plante. First, Syl gave him a lunge to his right and then a lunge to his left. I could see Plante thinking 'I've got him' and put his stick out for the puck. But then Syl deked him again, and it made bubbles inside me. It was the most beautiful goal I'd seen in a long time."

Apps quickly matured into one of the most artistic centers in the game. He finished the 1970–71 season in Pittsburgh, scoring nine goals and 16 assists for 25 points in 31 games. The following year, he played in 72 games, scoring 15 goals and 44 assists for 59 points. By contrast, Sather was a

Syl Apps of the Los Angeles Kings leads a rush.

15

seldom-used player in New York. Syl made Pittsburgh General Manager Jack Riley look like a genius. Riley, in turn, was tickled to have an Apps in his lineup.

"That was the best trade I ever made, even though it was my first one," Kelly recalls. "Syl really impressed me. In fact, he's got moves that some of the NHL's best centers don't have."

Riley defended the Rangers for making the seemingly one-sided trade: "I think it's possible to understand their reasoning. They already had three centers. It wasn't likely that Syl would replace one of them. What New York needed was a 'disturber' who would get the opposing team riled up. Sather fit that role. So the deal made sense from the Rangers' viewpoint. I don't know whether Apps could have played a wing position for them. He seems to belong at center—and that's where he makes things happen. Besides, I don't think anybody knew Syl would turn out to be such a fine hockey player. If the Rangers knew then what they know now, they wouldn't have made the trade."

Syl I also found favor with the trade. "My son didn't get enough ice time in New York," says the elder Apps. "I was pleased he was traded to Pittsburgh because Red Kelly, in my estimation, was one of the outstanding NHL coaches."

Kelly actually had played against the elder Apps for one season and Red detected a similarity in style between father and son. "Syl doesn't skate as fast as

his dad," Red says. "Busting out of his own end, Syl Sr. could really hunch his shoulders and go. But I think maybe young Syl handles the puck a bit better. Physically, the kid is just as strong."

Syl II got his first taste of Stanley Cup hockey in the 1972 playoffs, but his debut was shortened as the Penguins were eliminated in four straight games. The development of the Pittsburgh ace continued the following year as Syl scored 29 goals and 56 assists for 85 points. Clearly, his forte is his outstanding playmaking ability.

"I've always been the kind of forward who liked to set up my linemates," explains Apps. "I know I should shoot more, but sometimes, you just don't want to shoot."

Syl's equilibrium was disturbed in 1973 when coach Kelly left the Penguins and Ken Schinkel took over the floundering team. One of the few bright spots for Schinkel was Syl's consistent play. "The thing Syl has going for him," Schinkel says, "is that he never stops. He has great determination to get the puck. If he thinks he has any kind of chance to get there, he'll go for it."

Despite Syl's efforts, Pittsburgh failed to qualify for the Stanley Cup playoffs. By contrast, his former team, the Rangers, continued to ice one of the best teams in the league. Did Syl suffer any regrets? "For

Syl Apps, then with the Penguins, charges through the goal mouth.

16

quite some time the Rangers had the same three centers they had when they dealt me to Pittsburgh. Considering that fact, the trade was the best thing that could have happened to me. After all, it got my career under way."

Syl's extraordinary efforts inspired the rival World Hockey Association to take notice and when his contract with the Penguins expired, the WHA entered the bidding war for his services. The WHA's Toronto Toros made a stunning offer that tempted Syl. After all, signing with the Toros would have given Syl an opportunity to play in Toronto where the name Syl Apps had been a legend for decades.

But Syl II decided to stay in Pittsburgh and signed a new five-year contract for an estimated $750,000.

During the 1973–74 season, Syl scored 24 goals, and had 61 assists, mostly skimming passes to linemates Jean Pronovost and Lowell MacDonald. The trio led all lines in the NHL in scoring except for the Boston Bruins' Phil Esposito–Ken Hodge–Wayne Cashman triumvirate.

The Penguins added still more offense for the 1974–75 season by acquiring veterans Vic Hadfield and Rick Kehoe. Backed by solid goaltending from Gary Inness and Michel Plasse, the Pens made the playoffs and Apps continued his consistent play with 24 goals and 55 assists. Syl was named the outstanding player in the 1975 All-Star game.

Meanwhile, the Toronto Maple Leafs, in search of scoring punch, attempted to obtain Syl, offering goalie Doug Favell to the defensively poor Penguins. Jack Button, who then was Pittsburgh's manager, nixed the deal. "We never even considered the Favell–Apps deal seriously," says Button.

By this time Apps had become a household word among Pittsburgh hockey fans. During the 1975 playoffs Syl was involved in one of the strangest ironies in the sport's history. After eliminating the St. Louis Blues in the preliminary round, the Penguins moved on to meet the New York Islanders. Pittsburgh won the first three games of the best-of-seven series and appeared to be a shoo-in to advance to the semifinals. In fact, only one team in NHL history ever had rebounded from a 0–3 games deficit—and that was Syl Apps I's 1942 Toronto Maple Leafs who upset the Detroit Red Wings in the Stanley Cup finals. Certainly history would not repeat itself in so cruel a fashion for the younger Apps.

But the Islanders did counterattack successfully, winning the fourth game at Nassau Coliseum. Long Island then won its first game ever in Pittsburgh's Civic Arena to cut the games margin to 3–2. The Islanders returned to the Coliseum, tied the series, then completed the "miracle" with a late-goal, 1–0 victory in Pittsburgh.

The trauma notwithstanding, Apps recovered and enjoyed his finest season during the 1975–76 campaign, scoring career highs of 32 goals and 67 assists for 99 points. He had, by now, silenced all critics who ever suggested that young Syl never could wear the elder Syl's skates.

On November 1, 1977, Apps was surprisingly dealt to the Los Angeles Kings, with the Penguins receiving tough guy Dave Schultz and Gene Carr, as well as a draft choice. After seven seasons of personal success, along with the frustration of playing on a perennially mediocre club, Syl II hopes that, in Los Angeles, he can duplicate his father's accomplishment of playing on a Stanley Cup winner.

Despite the change of teams, Apps continued to star. On Saturday night, November 26, 1977, taking over for the Kings' injured star Marcel Dionne, he led L.A. to a 4–4 tie in Atlanta's Omni, scoring twice, including the game-tying goal in the final minute.

Whether Syl can help lead the Kings to a Stanley Cup remains to be seen. But whatever happens, Syl Apps has made his greatest fan very happy. "I've had excitement in hockey," says Syl Aps I, "but one of my proudest accomplishments has been watching my son make a success of himself. I can't think of a bigger thrill than I got watching Sylvanus score two goals in the All-Star game and win that car as the best player of the night."

Just a chip off the old block.

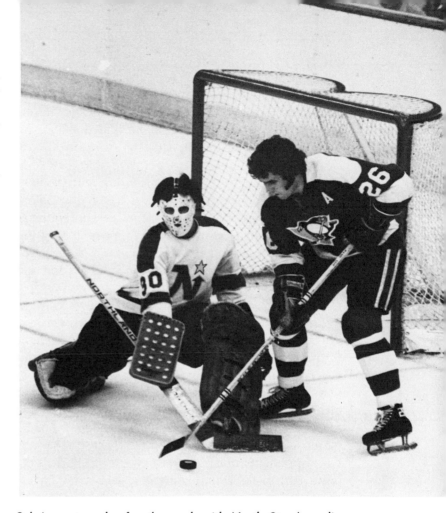

Syl Apps struggles for the puck with North Stars' goalie Cesare Maniago.

BOBBY CLARKE

All the odds were stacked against Bobby Clarke's becoming a successful professional hockey player. He discovered at age 15 that he had diabetes; he was also informed that he suffered from myopic vision, making it difficult to perceive things at long range. As a teenager, Clarke's skating and shooting skills were, at best, only average. Yet today Bobby Clarke ranks as one of the most successful National Hockey League Players—a three-time winner of the Hart Trophy, presented to the league's Most Valuable Player. Further, he has twice captained the Philadelphia Flyers to Stanley Cup championships.

Clarke's boyish face lends him a deceptively innocent image. However, once he puts on his uniform he is all business. His silver skate blades chop through the ice at full tilt every second he leads the Flyers. Unlike the league's more graceful performers, Clarke requires a tremendous effort because of his short choppy strides. Nevertheless, he always seems to be in the middle of the most rugged action, in the corners or behind and in front of the net. And opponents must always beware of Clarke's elbows and stick, which sometimes are a bit higher than the hockey law allows. When it comes to stick versus stick on faceoffs, Clarke is unbeatable.

Robert Earle Clarke was born and raised in the mining town of Flin Flon, Manitoba, just below the Arctic Circle. There was one thing on young Bobby's mind—hockey, hockey, and more hockey.

His mother, Yvonne Clarke, recalls, "Bobby learned to skate at Lakeside Park in Flin Flon. It had an open-air rink and he lived there, morning, noon, and night. As long as there was ice, he'd be out there practicing.

"Of course, that still wasn't enough hockey for him so we had another rink built out in the garden. Many's the time he'd shoot the puck off the side of the house—and a few times through the windows."

Bobby got his first taste of the excitement of competitive hockey when, in 1957, he saw Flin Flon's Junior Bombers defeat the Hull-Ottawa Canadiens to win the Memorial Cup, emblematic of Canada's junior hockey championship. One can picture the eight-year-old Clarke watching the Bombers' glorious victory and imagining himself out on the ice, in a Bombers' uniform. That, however, was still nine years of hard work away.

Clarke's first coach was Earl Garinger, who tutored him when Bobby was eight. At the time, Garinger seriously doubted that he was looking at a future NHL ace. "He was a strange skater," Garinger remembers. "Most kids who start out have trouble with their ankles bending in, but only one of Bobby's ankles *bent out*! This worried his dad a great deal. I told his father not to worry, that the ankle would straighten itself out in time; and it did."

But three years later, Garinger coached Bobby

again, and he noticed little progress in Clarke's hockey skills. "He hadn't changed much. He was a more or less average hockey player then. You would certainly never have guessed he'd be a future star."

Bobby didn't exactly agree with the assessment and worked to ascend the ladder to the Bombers, but at the age of 15 he suffered a setback that would have ended most youngster's hockey careers; he learned he was diabetic. It should have stopped him in his tracks.

Philadelphia Flyers' team physician Dr. Stanley Spoont of Lankenau Hospital explains the problems of a diabetic player: "There are several ways in which diabetes can affect an athlete. First, if his blood sugar is not normal, his immediate performance is affected. If the blood sugar is too low, for example, he would act peculiar, as though he had lost his coordination. He might have a fainting spell or a convulsion on the ice. If his blood sugar was too high, this would also affect his activity, in that muscles would not perform well. The skates would be very heavy for him."

The Clarkes were naturally worried about their son's health. "But it turned out we were a lot more concerned than Bobby was," says Mrs. Clarke. "Then we thought about it and realized that he was so healthy; he had never been sick; took good care of himself and never missed any games; so his hockey playing was okay with us."

Bobby Clarke, master of the face-off circle

21

In the autumn of 1966, at the age of 17, Bobby finally graduated to the Bombers. It was, in its way, a major accomplishment. Joining the Bombers meant a significant commitment for a Flin Flon lad since the nearest opponent is a 500-mile bus ride away. Playing for the Bombers meant that Bobby, like all members of the team, had to quit school to devote full time to hockey.

"It came down to this," explains his mother. "By the time Bobby was 17, he was going to the rink more than he was going to school."

The Bombers' coach Pat Ginnell remembers his first impressions of Bobby Clarke: "He was wearing glasses, and looked kind of thin when he got on the ice. But once he started moving, there was no doubt in my mind that this was going to be one of the best kids I ever coached."

Ginnell put Bobby on a line with a teenaged Canadian-Indian named Reggie Leach with fantastic results. "He never played a bad game for me," recalls Ginnell. "Never. Once Bobby started to fill out there was no stopping him."

Clarke exploded during the 1967–68 season, recording 51 goals and 117 assists for 168 points— all in a 59-game season. But Bobby was exhibiting another quality besides scoring ability that would make him such a valuable NHL player: unequivocal leadership.

"He started raging at his teammates during one terrible practice session," Ginnell says. "And I just let him go. I can still see him and hear him. . . . Clarkie said, 'I want to play hockey for a living and you guys are hurting me and the team by not working. So shape up!'" This was vintage Clarke.

The 1968–69 season was to be Bobby's final year of junior hockey, after which he would be eligible for the NHL draft. Ginnell realized that Clarke wanted to play professionally, but he also knew that word of his diabetic condition had spread, and the coach decided to do something about it. Prior to the start of the season, Ginnell took Bobby to the famed Mayo Clinic in Rochester, Minnesota. Ginnell remembers: "I figured that there was only one thing to do and that was to have the best doctors determine just how bad, or good, his health really was and what kind of future he might have as a big-league player."

The Mayo Clinic medics agreed that as long as Bobby took care of himself, there was no reason why he couldn't play professionally. Better still, the physicians gave Ginnell a letter that he could show to any NHL scouts who happened to visit Flin Flon in search of talent.

Clarke scored 51 goals and 86 assists for 137 points during his last year with the Bombers, but despite such impressive statistics and the letter from the Mayo Clinic, most NHL teams were reluctant to take a chance on signing him.

However, Gerry Melnyk, an administrative assistant in the Philadelphia Flyers' front office, and a

The heart and soul of the Flyers, Captain Bobby Clarke

man regarded as a perceptive judge of young talent, was very enthusiastic about Clarke. Melnyk suggested that the Flyers gamble on Clarke, but General Manager Bud Poile first wanted to consult with Dr. Spoont, the club physician. The doctor informed Poile that, as long as the youngster was cooperative, which he was, then there would be no problem. Still, the Flyers were reluctant to pick Clarke first in the draft and opted instead for a 6-6 giant named Bob Currier, much to Melnyk's dismay.

When it came time for the Flyers' second round selection, Clarke was still available. Both the Montreal Canadiens and the Detroit Red Wings, anticipating that the Flyers might select Clarke, tried to make a deal for Philadelphia's pick in advance.

"Jimmy Skinner (head Red Wings scout) told me that he'd give us a couple of pros for Clarke," said then Flyers' Assistant Manager Keith Allen. "I knew he realized he had made a mistake not picking Bobby ahead of us."

So, Bobby Clarke became a Philadelphia Flyer.

It was with some reluctance that Bobby left his home town of twenty years to report to the Flyers' training camp in Quebec City, but there was no homesickness in him once he laced on his first NHL skates.

Coach Vic Stasiuk placed Clarke on a line with rugged old Reggie Fleming and rookie Lew Morrison. Although the unit clicked almost immediately,

Bobby Clarke prevents a goal with his netminder out of position.

Bobby frightened the Flyers when he collapsed in the dressing room after a scrimmage. Flyer's officials were relieved to learn that Clarke's fainting spells were brought on by his skipping breakfast pior to the workouts.

At the Flyers' insistence, Bobby worked out a routine with trainer Frank Lewis whereby he would sip a cup of cola with two or three tablespoons of sugar in it before each game, and drink half a glass of sweetened orange juice between periods. The formula worked and in his rookie season, Bobby scored 15 goals and 31 assists for 46 points. More than that, he displayed enough potential to prompt Bud Poile to predict: "In three years Clarke will be the best in the NHL. And if he's not the best, I'll guarantee you he'll be among the top three."

Bobby displayed the class that gained him respect of teammate and foe alike. After winning a cash player-of-the-month award, Clarke donated the gift to Assistant Trainer Warren Elliot, whose daughter required heart surgery.

The Flyers did not make the playoffs that year, losing out in the last game of the season, 1–0, when goalie Bernie Parent missed an easy long shot by Minnesota North Stars' Barry Gibbs in the third period.

A year later Clarke scored 27 goals and 36 assists for 63 points while leading the Flyers to a third-place finish.

"The big thing is that my all-around play improved as well as my statistics," says Clarke. "But I'm not satisfied. I don't think a player should be. Though I've learned a lot, I'm learning more every time out."

Although the Flyers were successful in their playoff bid, they were quickly ousted in four straight Stanley Cup games by the Chicago Black Hawks. The rout was a disappointment for Clarke and the Flyers, but it was nothing compared to the misery of the 1971–72 season.

For Bobby the season was a personal triumph. He enjoyed an outstanding third pro season, with 35 goals and 46 assists for 81 points and his driving play prompted new coach Fred Shero to bluntly state: "Bobby Clarke could possibly be the greatest player in hockey today." Unfortunately, the Flyers took the gloss off such glowing triumphs. Needing only a tie to clinch a playoff spot in their final game of the season at Buffalo, the Flyers nursed a 2–2 score as the clock ticked down the closing seconds. But a former Philadelphia skater named Gerry Meehan collected the puck at the center red line, skated toward daylight and unleashed a long shot that beat Flyers' goalie Doug Favell with only four seconds to go. The Flyers were out of the playoffs.

"I can't believe it," said a shocked Clarke. "I feel dead inside. Every time I close my eyes I keep seeing that goal. That's all I see . . . that goal. And to think, we were only four seconds away!"

The Flyers clearly needed inspiration to restore their winning ways and Clarke provided it. In 1971–72 Bobby was named winner of the Bill Masterton Trophy as the player "who best exemplifies the qualities of perseverance, sportsmanship, and dedication to hockey." Clarke received another honor prior to the 1972–73 season when he was chosen to play for Team Canada, a professional All-Star team, in its eight-game series with the Soviet Union. Bobby was among the first players selected by coach Harry Sinden and now was among the *crème de la crème* of hockey.

"I had never been so nervous since the day I got married," says Clarke. "This was the biggest thing that ever happened to me in sports. I was proud to have the opportunity to play for something more than money. There was so much more at stake in that series. We were representing our country and finally getting the chance to prove that we are what we believe we are—the best in the world."

Sinden placed Clarke on a line between two Toronto Maple Leaf forwards, right wing Ron Ellis and left wing Paul Henderson. The result was, in the words of *Toronto Star* reporter Frank Orr, "the cohesion of a line which has worked together for several seasons. In Team Canada's scheme they ranked as the most consistent two-way troika, producing goals and excelling defensively."

Sinden recalls: "The Clarke line was the surprise of our training camp. Not that we didn't expect them to do well. It's just that we didn't expect such consistency. They complemented each other, and we lucked into it. All three can skate. And all three take care of themselves; so they came to camp in shape."

With Canada's national honor at stake, the mighty Team Canada was expected to sweep the eight-game series; the first four games to be played in Canada and then four in Russia. But Team Canada left North America with a disappointing 1–2–1 mark and a sendoff of boos from angry Vancouver fans. After losing the first game in Moscow, Team Canada courageously rallied to win the final three games and the series, when Clarke's linemate Paul Henderson scored the winning goal in the eighth game with only 19 seconds remaining in the third period.

Bobby Clarke confers with teammate Reg Leach.

Although they won the series, the eight-game showdown was less than a triumph for Team Canada; it was, however, quite a feather in Bobby Clarke's hat.

"My confidence was reinforced quite a bit," Bobby reflects. "Before I played with the guys from Team Canada, I wasn't sure I belonged on the ice with them. I was always in awe of people like Phil Esposito and Brad Park. But once we got on the ice together I became much more confident and pretty soon I felt I could play as well as the rest of them.

"The Russians proved to me that they really are great hockey players. Personally, I'd like to play them again. Whether I do or not, the series in September 1972 will never be forgotten, particularly the games in Moscow. I truly felt I was playing for Canada's national honor."

Sinden unequivocally says that Team Canada never could have done as well without Clarke. But the most heartwarming praise came from Soviet coach Boris Kulagin: "Clarke fits the mold of the best type of hockey player, because apart from his wonderful skill, he is completely unselfish and a complete team player. Canada had more dominant players, yet I think none was more valuable than Clarke. Many players never stop trying, but they waste motion and effort. Clarke never does this."

Bobby's perseverance and grim determination revitalized the Flyers in the 1972–73 season and Clarke was named captain of the team. The result was a new personal career high of 37 goals and 67 assists for 104 points as the Flyers finished second to Chicago in the NHL's West Division.

Clarke lauded his mates, saying: "You have to have some good hockey players to finish second. Everybody has built us up to be just a rough team. It's not so. And I don't think intimidation is a factor in our success. Not in the playoffs. Hitting, yes, but not intimidation. The overall play of our team helped each player individually. I found that I was let alone more than in the past because anytime someone bothered me, someone on the Flyers went after him."

For his efforts, Clarke was presented the Hart Trophy as the NHL's Most Valuable Player. This was the first time a West Division player had won the award. "Clarke got only 37 goals while our Rick MacLeish scored 50 and Bill Flett scored 43," recalls Coach Shero. "Yet, no one thought anyone but Bobby was our MVP."

Clarke's tenacious style inspired admiration from friend and foe alike. Toronto Maple Leafs' Captain Darryl Sittler says: "Clarke does anything he can to make you think of something other than playing your game. A little whack here, a little jab there. If he can't get you upset, he just steps up the nonsense until he does, and some of it is pretty tough. Cripes, he wants to win so badly that he'll do just about anything."

Clarke's diligence paid dividends as the Flyers swept to two consecutive Stanley Cup victories. In 1973–74, Bobby scored 35 goals and 52 assists for 87 points as Philadelphia won the West Division pennant and went on to stun the New York Rangers in the semifinals and crush the Boston Bruins in the Stanley Cup finals.

Bobby scored the most important goal of the Flyers' playoff crusade after Philadelphia had lost the first game of the finals at Boston Garden in heart-breaking fashion when the Bruins' Bobby Orr scored in the last minute to give Boston a 3–2 victory.

The Flyers needed to win the second game to gain a split of the two games in Boston, but the Bruins nursed a 2–1 lead as the teams headed into the final minute of play.

With 52 seconds left in regulation time, defenseman Andre Dupont tied the score, sending the game into sudden-death overtime. Then Captain Clarke took command, snared the puck near the Boston goal and, after two swipes, put the puck over the red line.

Philadelphia's heroes were numerous. Flawless goaltending by Bernie Parent, the high-powered offense of Bill Barber and Rick MacLeish, and the muscle of Dave Schultz and Don Saleski helped turn the series around, but it was the indefatigable Clarke who provided the irreplaceable inspiration.

Bobby contributed in other ways to the Flyers second cup victory, achieved in a six-game triumph over the Buffalo Sabres. Prior to the 1974–75 season, Clarke recommended that Philadelphia obtain his former Flin Flon (Junior) Bombers' linemate Reggie Leach. President Ed Snider took his advice, and Leach, who had been a monumental disappointment with the California Golden Seals and the Boston Bruins, was inserted on Clarke's line and promptly scored 45 big NHL goals.

In the final series with Buffalo, the Flyers, after sweeping two games at the Philadelphia Spectrum, lost the next two games at the Memorial Auditorium in Buffalo. It was time for Clarke to bring his leadership to the fore. "The Philadelphia locker room was closed for 15 minutes after the fourth game," says a Flyers' official, "because Bobby was lashing the rest of the Flyers verbally, telling them how stupid it was to get that far in the playoffs and then throw all the gains away."

The Flyers rallied to win the next two games and their second straight Stanley Cup. Clarke was voted winner of the Hart Trophy for the second time, having scored 27 goals and 89 assists for 116 points.

Bobby also won the Hart Trophy for the 1975–76 season with a 30-goal, 89 assist effort, although the Flyers lost the Stanley Cup finals to the powerful Montreal Canadiens in four straight games.

In the 1976–77 season Bobby scored 27 goals and 63 assists for 90 points. A year later he had 21 goals and 68 assists for a commendable 89 points.

Win or lose, the Flyers have remained one of the NHL's most dynamic clubs thanks to their captain, who is appreciated by the stickboy as much as by the club owner. Flyers' President Ed Snider puts it this way: "People tend to exaggerate the superstar thing, so you'll just have to take my word for it. Clarke is *it*. He's not just an amazing hockey player. He's an amazing human being, a once-in-a-lifetime-guy."

Bobby Clarke scores a wrap-around goal against the Maple Leafs.

MARCEL DIONNE

Who is 5-9, 170 pounds, purple and gold, able to dart around the ice like a water bug on a pond, and is called "Little Beaver" of the NHL?

None other than Marcel Dionne of the Los Angeles Kings, who also is one of the league's most accurate shooters. Dionne's 1976–77 totals of 53 goals and 69 assists for 122 points placed him second in scoring behind the Montreal Candiens' gifted Guy Lafleur.

The development of Dionne is an example of a despondent athlete who finally found happiness after four turbulent seasons with the Detroit Red Wings and a pressure-packed first year (1975–76) with the Kings.

Marcel grew up in the steel mill town of Drummondville, in the mostly French-speaking province of Quebec. Born on August 3, 1951, Marcel required only two years before he began skating on a makeshift rink in his backyard. His parents encouraged young Marcel to play hockey, aware that if he didn't make a career of hockey, he inevitably would spend his life working in the steel mills, like his father.

As a result, the Dionnes saw to it that their son's hockey thirst always was quenched.

"When I needed some equipment," Marcel recalls, "I would have it. No matter how bad the times were for my family, my parents made sure I had the best. And my uncles, some of them were single then, they also would get hockey things for me. When I was 13 years old, I already had $55 skates. That was like owning a Rolls-Royce."

When Marcel was 15, he had established himself as a professional prospect and he had outgrown Drummondville. It was time for him to move on to the big time and play for the Montreal Junior Canadiens, one of the strongest amateur teams in all Canada.

"It was hard to leave home at that age," says Dionne, "but I went to Montreal and made new friends."

The move to Montreal also was part of the price of wanting to make it to the pros. Dionne played spectacularly for his new club, and after his rookie season he received an invitation to play for the St. Catharines Ontario Junior A team, a club that had developed and sent such stars as Bobby Hull and Stan Mikita to the majors. Dionne accepted the offer although St. Catharines was in Ontario, where only English was spoken. Since Marcel could only speak French, he had catapulted himself into a very awkward situation.

"At first, I had to listen to every English word I said," Dionne remembers. "Then, I got so I could speak English without listening to every word. Now it's like my first language."

During his three year pro apprenticeship at St. Catharines, Marcel established a career Ontario

Hockey Association scoring record of 375 points. He attracted attention throughout Canada and NHL clubs scouted the mighty little scoring machine as if they had found a gold mine of goals. In fact, Dionne was so highly regarded that he was selected second in the 1971 NHL amateur draft by the Detroit Red Wings; only Guy Lafleur of the Canadiens was chosen before Dionne. Desperate for help, the Red Wings expected instant miracles from Marcel. Detroit General Manager Ned Harkness sought a replacement for the legendary Gordie Howe, who had quit the Wings following the 1970–71 season (only to later return as an active player for the Houston Aeros). But Gordie Howe replacements are seldom found.

Dionne hired super-attorney Alan Eagleson to negotiate his contract, and the result was a pact that Eagleson labelled "the best I've ever negotiated for a rookie . . . better even than the original one I negotiated for Bobby Orr with the Boston Bruins."

Along with big money, Dionne received unprecedented attention from the Detroit press and the fans, who expected the kind of results that a six-figure contract suggests.

Consequently Dionne found himself in a pressure cooker atmosphere before he even put on a Red Wings' uniform.

"When you are 18 years old and playing junior hockey," Dionne says, "you do not think of pressure; the game is fun. Then all of a sudden you are

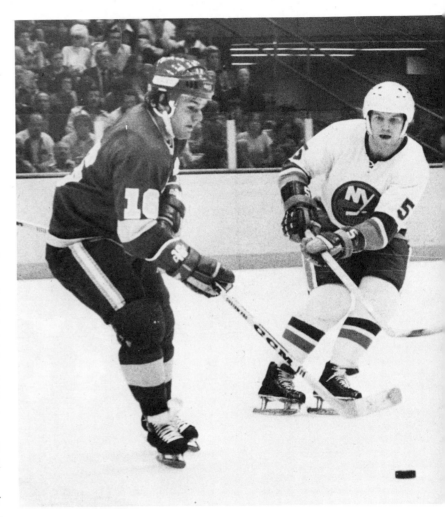

Marcel Dionne and Denis Potvin chase a loose puck.

Marcel Dionne at the goal mouth

drafted by an NHL team, and everything changes."

As an NHL rookie Dionne suffered his first trauma during the exhibition season. He scored a paltry two goals, and the press promptly needled him. "Whatever happened to the Red Wings' number one draft choice?" was a typical media barb. The kid who only a year earlier had been overwhelmed with adulation now was the subject of ruthless scorn.

"It was more difficult in the NHL than I imagined," Dionne says. "There was such a big difference in the style of play; it is so much faster in the majors. I had scoring chances as a rookie, but I just couldn't connect. My teammates told me not to miss on those kind of chances in this league. They are so much quicker and the checking is quicker, and then there is the pressure because here you are playing for money: big money."

Red Wings' coach Doug Barkley defended and shielded his prize 20-year-old rookie. "I'm not disappointed with Marcel," Barkley said at the time. "He's improving with each game. He can skate. He can shoot. He has all the moves. But he must learn the difference between the NHL and junior hockey. And, mark my words, he will!"

Dionne did, but Barkley was not around to savor the enjoyment. Harkness had replaced him with Johnny Wilson, who gave Marcel added responsibilities. The new coach put Dionne on the sputtering Detroit power play—with splendid results. "He's been a big asset to our power play," Wilson said.

"Marcel is very creative with the puck. He forces his teammates into the openings. It appears to me that he actually has fun on the power play; that he really likes to take advantage of the other team being a man short. He works on the opposition defense. He's got quick moves and a great shift, and he doesn't stand around. He's got a hell of a shot . . . and he can give you the kind of end-to-end rush that lifts a power play. He's hard to check because he's so shifty that he can duck under the opposition. If Marcel was taller, it might work against him."

Dionne overcame the pressures of his freshman year, and gradually appeared to be the second coming of Gordie Howe after all.

Marcel completed his rookie season with 28 goals and 49 assists for 77 points, a new NHL record for points in a season by a rookie. Thus, it hardly was surprising that he received a veteran's responsibility. "I invariably put him against the best centers in the league," said Coach Wilson. "He goes against the guys like Phil Esposito, Dave Keon, Jean Ratelle and Gil Perreault and holds his own or does better than the best of the veterans."

For inexplicable reasons, Dionne finished a distant third in the voting for the Calder Trophy, given to the NHL's outstanding rookie. Marcel placed behind Buffalo's Richard Martin, who scored 44 goals, and Montreal's lawyer-goalie Ken Dryden. The rejection of Dionne inspired a hail of protest, especially in Detroit.

"My guy's a two-way player," said an angry

Johnny Wilson. "He passes, he can skate, and he can handle the puck. The other guy (Martin) just stands there in front of the net and blasts the puck through everybody."

Although the silverware eluded him, Marcel did win a reputation as a potent scorer and playmaker but he also was fast becoming notorious as a troublemaker. The first negative incident occurred when Dionne overslept and missed the Red Wings' team plane for Minnesota. It was the first time in ten years a Red Wing had committed so egregious a sin. Marcel was punished with a stiff fine from Wilson.

The anti-Dionne claque also was quick to point out that, despite the presence of Marcel, the Red Wings managed to miss the playoffs that year (as well as each of the four years Dionne remained in Detroit). As Red Wings' losses mounted throughout Marcel's second and third seasons in the Motor City, Dionne was singled out by management as "l'enfant terrible" of the team. The bosses accused him of "not giving one hundred percent" and not being a team player. Marcel himself fanned the flames of dissension with such comments as: "There are only three NHL-caliber players on this team." And he himself admitted that he was holding back. "I'm not going to give one hundred percent in practice," he said. "I don't believe in the theory that practice makes perfect. I think it can only hurt a player if he skates his very best in practice." This philosophy put Dionne on a collision course with

Manager Ned Harkness, whose rah-rah attitude was a carryover from his days as a college hockey coach. Even Coach Wilson became disenchanted with Dionne one day at a morning practice session before a night game against the Vancouver Canucks. The coach noticed that Dionne was skating leisurely. Furious, Wilson summoned Marcel to the sideboards. "He was all fired up and told me to start skating," Dionne recalls. "I spoke to him and told him that I felt there wasn't really any reason for me to break my chops in practice. . . . Well, he told me to leave and not to come back. I left the ice, and I *didn't* come back!"

Indeed, Marcel managed to miss that night's game and was promptly suspended.

Despite such dilemmas, Dionne enjoyed an outstanding offensive year, with 40 goals and 50 assists for 90 points. Detroit management could not argue with such statistics, but Marcel remained subject to harsh criticism.

"Harkness thought Marcel wasn't going all out," Wilson later recalled, "and he thought Marcel should put more effort into forechecking. The suspension was blown out of proportion. I was irritated; I had just had my head blown off by Ned, and I took it out on Dionne. . . . I agree with Dionne that a practice session should be a form of relaxation. How much can your body take, right?"

In Marcel's third season irascible Ted Garvin took over as head coach, and instantly there was a personality clash. Garvin accused the young center of loafing, and Dionne responded by demanding to be traded.

"You don't see the Bobby Orrs and Phil Espositos complaining about everything and not working," Garvin said. "You don't see the very best players cackling like hens at everything that happens during a hockey season. Dionne is only looking to make a fast million bucks. He doesn't care about winning. He only cares about himself and paychecks."

By now the troubles were having a telling effect. Dionne slumped off to a disappointing 24-goal year.

The 1974–75 season, Dionne's fourth in the majors, brought yet another new head coach, this time former Detroit superstar Alex Delvecchio. But more importantly, it was Marcel's option year—by not signing a new contract, Dionne would be free to go to the team of his choice at the end of the campaign. Knowing this, the Red Wings attempted to make Marcel happy by giving him still more responsibility. In a shocking move, Dionne was named team captain.

"The captain bit was a big surprise to me," said Dionne. "Mickey Redmond, I guess, said it best— he said that it wasn't bad going from the doghouse to captain. Now the Red Wings expect leadership from me. Fine. But I'll do the same things I've always done. I'm going to be the same man.

"With all the problems I've had, I'm surprised

Marcel Dionne on a rush

35

they wanted me to be captain. I guess it's just because I've got a big mouth."

Playing like the Dionne of old, Marcel had his finest season as a Red Wing, amassing 47 goals and 74 assists for 121 points, placing him behind only Phil Esposito and Bobby Orr in the NHL scoring race.

But the productive campaign failed to erase the scars of bygone years and, once the season ended, Eagleson informed Delvecchio that Dionne would be taking his services elsewhere.

"We offered him a four year contract for a million—$250,000 per year," said Delvecchio. "But he thinks he can get more money somewhere else. He said he didn't want to play in Detroit anymore. He said 'the name of the game is money' and he thinks he can get more money somewhere else. Personally, I think Dionne is a pretty selfish individual. Now it looks as though what he did for the Red Wings last year was all for himself." And so the big question: who would sign Marcel for 1975–76?

Six teams were in the early running—Montreal Canadiens, St. Louis Blues, Buffalo Sabres, Toronto Maple Leafs, Los Angeles Kings, and Edmonton Oilers (of the WHA). Dionne's demands were high, as were the Red Wings', who were entitled to compensation from the team that signed Marcel. Ultimately, the Kings, whose owner Jack Kent Cooke had just acquired Kareem Abdul-Jabbar for his basketball Lakers, offered the most money.

The Kings won the bidding war, and surrendered

Marcel Dionne cranks up a slapshot.

36

veteran defenseman Terry Harper and rugged forward Dan Maloney to Detroit. Cooke signed Marcel to a five-year, $1.5 million pact.

Although Dionne and Cooke danced cartwheels of joy, Kings' Coach Bob Pulford unhappily muttered that the deal was not in the best interests of his club. Under Pulford's disciplined defensive style, the Kings previously had enjoyed an extremely successful season. Los Angeles had the fourth best won–lost record in the league, and only the Stanley Cup champion Philadelphia Flyers allowed fewer goals. Terry Harper had been the captain of the squad and the leader on defense. Maloney, a muscular winger, could score goals and tend to checking. In Dionne, the Kings were adding a free-wheeling player whose style appeared conspicuously out of place in the Kings' system. Coach Pulford worried that Dionne might disrupt his previously sound club, both on and off the ice.

"I've told Marcel, and he knows it," Pulford explained, "that he can't float around center ice here the way he did in Detroit. He must retreat into the defensive end and work with the defenseman to get the puck out. This type of discipline is new to him, and I know it will take time for him to learn our system."

But Pulford added hopefully: "Dionne may be the best forward in the NHL. There's no doubt he's a valuable addition to our club."

The "Little Beaver" was up to the new challenge in California. "Everything I do here with LA is important," he said. "The little things mean more—holding your man, just standing in front of him—things that the average person doesn't notice. They never mattered in Detroit.

"There's so much more enthusiasm here and a much bigger challenge. I feel like I want to play every game.

"I won't be doing just one job—scoring. I'll play more conservatively. Don't misunderstand me, I won't change my style too much. I just won't get caught up ice."

To make sure Dionne didn't get caught up ice, Pulford immediately assigned Marcel to the "fat squad," thinking that his ever-present paunch was a bit bigger than usual. ("I've always had a big stomach for a little guy. I like to eat. I'm a big hamburger man.") Pulford sent Dionne through rigorous stop-and-go skating drills following practice each day. The coach warned Marcel about dogging it in practice one day when Pulford noticed Dionne relaxing during training camp.

After a brief period of adjustment with his new team, Marcel settled down and scored 40 goals and 54 assists for 94 points. However, the Kings no longer were the stingy defensive team they had been the year before. They gave up more goals, and instead of battling Montreal for first place in the NHL's Norris Division, the club floundered far back of the leader.

Perhaps the toughest night of the entire 1975–76 season for Dionne occurred on his return to De-

Marcel Dionne pursues Yvan Cournoyer.

troit. The Dionneless Red Wings had been having trouble drawing people, but 14,500 fans turned out to "greet" the man who, in his four years as a Red Wing, had scored more points than any other four-year man in the history of the NHL. Dionne's "greeting" was a disheartening distillation of boos and vicious taunts. Frustrated by the jeers and by the persistent checking of the Red Wings' pesky Denis Polonich, the usually mild-mannered Dionne took a swipe at Polonich with his stick. At another point, he took a stiff check that knocked him down and sprained his arm. But he remained in the game.

"Marcel showed a lot of guts," says teammate Mike Corrigan. "He withstood a lot of abuse. He pushed himself on and showed us he wanted to win."

It was a tough adjustment for Dionne to adapt to the Kings' style, but he made the necessary changes and was ready for the 1976–77 season, only this time as a right wing.

Dionne became a new man, scoring goals, setting up teammates unselfishly, while diligently attending to the less glamorous job on defense. He was the only player to stay close to the Canadiens' Guy Lafleur in the scoring race. Marcel finished the 1976–77 season with 53 goals, 69 assists, and, for a pleasant change, rave reviews for his "new" positive attitude.

"He's the complete opposite of everything the Detroit people said he was," said former Kings General Manager Jake Milford. "In our games in Los Angeles he never wanted to be picked a star of the game and I don't even think he ever worried about the scoring race. He had become that much of a team player."

Montreal Canadiens' Coach Scotty Bowman is equally enthusiastic about Dionne. "If anything, he's too unselfish," says Bowman. "It's not as if he's just a shooter. He can make plays and sometimes I think he even prefers to make plays."

Milford believes that the move to right wing helped Marcel improve his defensive game. "He checks better on the wing," Milford explains, "because it's easier for him to pick up his winger. Marcel is also able to shoot more from the wing."

Unfortunately, Dionne's improvement failed to help the Kings cope with the powerful Canadiens in the 1977 Norris Division race. In the playoffs, the Kings again failed to get past the quarterfinal round, although they hung tough against the feisty Boston Bruins after losing the first three games—finally bowing in six.

And in 1977–78 Marcel led the Kings in scoring with 79 points in 70 games. With a happy Marcel Dionne, the Kings should now mean nothing but trouble to opponents in future seasons.

KEN DRYDEN

Rarely has a professional athlete burst on the major league scene with the distillation of charisma and culture the way Ken Dryden did during the 1971 Stanley Cup playoffs. A graduate of Cornell University, this native of Hamilton, Ontario, orbited from an unobtrusive job as part-time goalie for the American Hockey League's Montreal Voyageurs to the Most Valuable Player in the 1971 playoffs. His astonishing goaltending led the Montreal Canadiens—just an ordinary team throughout the regular season—past the powerful Boston Bruins to the Stanley Cup. Aided by a huge (6-4, 210 pounds) frame that amply fills the four by six feet net, Ken has established himself not only as a quality performer but also as a fascinating individual who worked for consumer advocate Ralph Nader in his spare time and pursued studies at law school as well.

Because of his size, Dryden is not the most agile goalie in the league—but neither is he the clumsiest. Ken is a "stand-up" goaltender; his most effective weapon is an agile glove (left) hand that caused nightmares for the Boston Bruins following the 1971 playoffs in which Dryden excelled. Although Ken is not regarded as a "roaming" goalie, he often catapults his teammates into break-out patterns from their own zone with clever passes. Once the play is in motion and the Canadiens control the puck in enemy zone, Dryden assumes an idiosyncratic pose, resting his hands and head atop his goalie stick.

How did this cerebral individual reach the top in the icy jungle of the NHL? The Dryden saga began on the streets of Islington, Ontario, a suburb of Toronto, where young, angular Ken played ball hockey using goals made of two-by-fours and chicken wire. "I played one goal and my older brother, Dave, played the other," recalls Ken. "That's all there was to it. We had tournaments every Saturday. Rubber balls were crummy on the pavement, but tennis balls were great. They stung more, too."

Despite the stings, bruises and assorted black-and-blue marks of the goaltending trade, Ken started playing competitively at age seven, with the Humber Valley Atoms. His shot-blocking came so naturally that, a year later, he moved up to the Humber Valley Peewees, although he was three years younger than most of his teammates. "My father put me in the advanced league intentionally," Ken explains. "His feeling was that I could improve more by playing against older boys. He was right because I always managed to do pretty well with the older fellows."

By the time he was 15, Ken was regarded as a legitimate pro hockey prospect. Most young Canadians would have been ecstatic at the possibilities but Ken was not enamoured with the thought of

Cerebral Ken Dryden of the Canadiens stands ready to stop a
shot.

becoming a professional athlete. True, he loved playing hockey, but school was the number one priority in the Dryden household. Ken proved the point when the lordly Montreal Canadiens came to him with an offer that most boys would not have been able to refuse. "Sorry," said Dryden, "but college comes first." He meant every word of it, and still does.

"They wanted me to play Junior A hockey— which was the fastest amateur league—in Peterborough, Ontario. But my schooling was the hang-up. I was planning to attend Grade 13, the most important academic year for a high school student in Canada. I realized at the time that there would be a lot of pressure on me to do well in the classroom. I couldn't see how living away, playing hockey and trying to go to school in Peterborough would work out for me, so I stayed in Toronto."

Always study-oriented, Dryden was disturbed by the manner in which youngsters were then quitting high school to play full-time junior hockey. To this day, he criticizes the syndrome: "The Canadian system of school vs. hockey is incredibly bad. Sure, it's okay for the guys who make it up to the NHL. But the majority of kids who leave school to play hockey never reach the top and get stuck with a 10th grade education anyway. As I see it, the idea is to mesh the hockey and education together, without lowering the quality of either. The tragedy is that this has so seldom been done."

Fortunately for Ken, he was able to find such a formula. In 1965, at age 18, Dryden enrolled at Cornell University. He ignored the many people who claimed that in going to Cornell he was giving up all chance to reach the NHL. Pro scouts had made it a practice of discouraging youths from attending American colleges. The scouts insisted that the quality of U.S. collegiate hockey was inferior to Canadian Junior A grade hockey. Scouts also pointed out that the college schedule was only 24 games long, contrasted to 70 games in Junior hockey.

Dryden brushed off the cynics and discovered that, yes, he did enjoy the short collegiate hockey schedule. It increased his concentration and enabled him to devote more time to his studies. "It's a definite advantage to have other interests besides hockey," Ken explains. "I used to play my worst games over Christmas vacation when I had nothing else to do. When you're involved in several things you sort of keep going—almost on nothing but nervous energy at times."

Dryden was a three-time All-American goalie for Cornell. He lost only four out of 83 career games, with an airtight goals-against average of 1.60 goals a game. Not surprisingly, he maintained an impressive academic record, with a high B average. But undergraduate studies were not enough to satisfy his thirst for knowledge. Ken wanted to go to law school and was accepted at prestigious Harvard

Montreal's Ken Dryden clears a rebound.

Law School. However, he decided against attending because Harvard wouldn't allow him to play hockey. Ken was confused, and torn between the pursuit of a law degree and a pro hockey career.

"It's funny," he says, "sometimes I felt impulses leading me to pro hockey and other times I thought I should simply go to law school and forget pro hockey altogether. One thing was certain—I knew I couldn't do both and expect to play meaningful hockey for the rest of my life."

Dryden returned to Canada and accepted an interesting offer from the Canadian National Hockey Team, which included full tuition at the University of Manitoba. On the surface at least, it appeared that Dryden was set for a few years, attending law school, and playing hockey as well. He was one person having his cake and eating it too. But the Canadian National Team folded a year later and Ken found himself with goalie pads but no place to wear them; that is, until the Montreal Canadiens, who had been waiting for a break such as this, moved in and made Ken an offer he couldn't refuse, signing Dryden to a two-year contract. Ken stipulated that he would not forsake his law studies. With that in mind Canadiens' Manager Sam Pollock agreed that Dryden would be a part-time player for the Montreal Voyageurs, then the Canadiens' farm club in the American League. He also would be able to continue law school at McGill University in Montreal.

Dryden attended the Canadiens' training camp in the fall of 1970, assured that he would be with the Voyageurs once the NHL season began. What Ken didn't bargain for was getting a taste of big-league hockey during exhibition games. He liked the taste and it set him thinking about playing in the NHL. When the season started, however, the Canadiens were well-established in goal with the veteran Rogatien Vachon and newcomer Phil Myre. "You know, getting into the exhibitions opened a new challenge," says Dryden. "I came to camp and on the first day it was downright frightening. Then it became interesting and then exciting. When you discover that you belong the experience stops being a lark, it becomes a challenge. So I began thinking of the big team. It came as a bit of a shock when I found I was left off. It called for a re-evaluation on my part."

After meeting with Canadiens' General Manager Sam Pollock, Dryden was satisfied that his—and Pollock's—original plans were in effect. Yes, the NHL *was* at least two years off.

"Now that we're back to the original plan," he said after meeting with Pollock, "I'm going to work at school. There was a point when I figured I'd come here, go to school, play with the Voyageurs and live happily ever after. But things changed in camp and it was a new perspective and, maybe, the big team became a possibility if not right away."

Dryden's agreement with the Canadiens allowed

him to attend only one practice a week for the Voyageurs, so that he could devote time to school. By Christmas, he had played in only five games.

"After Christmas," Dryden explains, "I had an easier schedule at the university, so I agreed to play full-time for the Voyageurs. This meant road trips to Cleveland, Springfield, and a few other places."

Ken played in 33 games for the Voyageurs, compiling an admirable 2.68 goals-against average, including three shutouts. It was impressive enough to persuade Pollock to invite Dryden to the NHL for a peek. As a result the Canadiens promoted Dryden to the big team on an emergency basis. Ken received permission to have his final examinations postponed until summer so he could remain with the NHL club for the remainder of the season. Many hockey reporters believed that Montreal merely was throwing Ken a bone—a couple of games of NHL experience—as they played out the schedule. The playoffs were soon coming and Vachon was expected back in the Montreal nets. No one thought the Canadiens would go with the rookie Dryden in the playoffs.

No one, that is, but Voyageurs' Coach Floyd Curry. He recalls: "I told Sammy Pollock when he took Dryden from us that he had just assured himself of a Stanley Cup. The kid was that good."

Meanwhile, Canadiens Coach Al MacNeil was more and more intrigued with Dryden's efforts in late-season games, first against the easier opponents. "They had me playing on the road against expansion teams," Dryden explains. "This meant there wasn't the tension for me that I might have felt if I had played at The Forum in Montreal. Within a few games I had a feel for NHL shooting and my only problem was learning to concentrate more intensely than I had been either in college hockey or the American League."

Playing in six regular season NHL games for the Canadiens, Dryden allowed only nine goals as Montreal finished the regular schedule in third place. The club had been plagued all year by injuries, including a severely broken leg suffered by defenseman Serge Savard. Considering the Canadiens' vulnerable spots, Montreal was not expected to get by first-place Boston, whom they were to meet in the initial round of the Stanley Cup playoffs.

Then came the first in a chain reaction of dramatic events. The Canadiens shocked the hockey world by announcing that Ken Dryden would be their *starting goalie* for the opening game against the Bruins in hostile Boston Garden. Playing in the Stanley Cup playoffs alone would be enough of an assignment for a 23-year-old rookie with a measly six games of major league experience; but Dryden was facing a Boston sextet that, led by superstars Bobby Orr and Phil Esposito, had scored 399 goals during the 78 game season.

The curtain lifted on the series as expected with Boston winning 3–1 at home. Dryden played well

Ken Dryden in control

but, obviously, not well enough. In the second game, also in The Hub, the Bruins rolled up a 5–1 lead and appeared certain of victory. But Dryden and the Canadiens rallied for an awesome 7–5 come-from-behind win. Again Dryden was less than spectacular but he kept the Canadiens alive.

The teams split the next two games in Montreal, but the Bruins took the fifth game. Montreal fought back and demolished the Bruins, 8–3, in the sixth game. Suddenly, Dryden and his Canadiens found themselves in remarkable position, just one win away from beating the Bruins out of the playoffs.

The seventh game at Boston Garden was Dryden's finest hour. The Habs took a 4–2 lead, and then let their goalie man the barricades where Dryden produced one spectacular save after another as Montreal delivered one of the greatest upsets in NHL history, dispatching the Bruins.

"Their entire team played well," remembers Phil Esposito, "but Dryden decided the series. He never cracked, never appeared to lose confidence or be bothered by the pressure. He beat us!" Esposito was robbed numerous times by Dryden, and several photographs taken during that game depict the former Boston sharpshooter looking to the roofs in disbelief after a spectacular save by the gangly Montreal rookie.

In the second round of the playoffs, the Canadiens survived a letdown and defeated the scrappy Minnesota North Stars in six games. Now Dryden and company had arrived in the finals, opposing the Chicago Black Hawks. Like the Boston series, this, too, went to the seventh and deciding game. Again Dryden faced the foe on the road, at Chicago Stadium. The Hawks jumped to a 2–0 lead in the final game, but the Canadiens counterattacked to go ahead 3–2. As they did in the last game of the Boston series, Montreal's forwards and defensemen appeared to sag while tacitly saying: "We'll let the kid, Dryden, do the rest." Ken *did* the rest and the Canadiens were Stanley Cup champs. To this day it remains one of the major upsets in sports history.

Playing in all twenty playoff games, Ken recorded a 3.00 goals-against average and was named the winner of the Conn Smythe Trophy as the most valuable player in the playoffs.

Instantly, experts began comparing Dryden to past goaltending greats. At 6-4 Dryden reminded observers of another tall Canadiens goalie of the 1940s—the inimitable, ambidextrous Bill Durnan. "The way Ken gets in front of shots to make impossible saves," says retired Habs' Captain Henri Richard, "he's a lot like Durnan used to be. Dryden murders you with surprise moves from seemingly impossible positions. It's great for a defenseman or a forward to know he's behind you."

Still there were those skeptics who wondered whether Dryden's springtime antics were some kind of a fluke. Would he be as good the following season? Sure enough, Dryden continued to baffle NHL shooters while maintaining his law studies.

During the off-season Dryden caused a sensation by taking a summer job working for consumer advocate Ralph Nader. "Actually, I worked more with environmental subjects than I did in the consumer area," Ken says. "But I'm interested in the broad area of public interests." When Ken returned to the NHL for full-time work, the Montreal management was concerned about his ability to combine law studies and a full-time big-league job. "It was more difficult my first year than it was in the second season," Dryden remembers. "The first year I had required courses that were given early in the morning when we had practice.

"In the second season I took elective courses and most of them were held later in the afternoon. My hockey day, when we didn't have a game, was finished at noon. The only difficult time was when exams came around—I didn't have as much time as I should have to prepare for them."

A serious academic-professional conflict developed at Christmas time. "We had a Western trip," Ken recalls, "that went from Sunday to Sunday, and I had exams just prior to the first Sunday, and one on the Tuesday after we came back. We also played Toronto that Wednesday night. It made my life a bit difficult but, somehow, I managed."

Without question, Dryden succeeded at both careers and at no time did his goaltending suffer in the 1971–72 season. Dryden compiled an outstanding 2.24 goals-against average, with eight shutouts. He was voted the winner of the Calder Trophy as Rookie of the Year—he was still "officially" a first-year man despite playing in 20 playoff games the previous season. The glorious bubble temporarily burst in the playoffs when the Canadiens were eliminated in the first round by the New York Rangers.

Wisps of disharmony began to appear around Ken's locker. When the 1971–72 season concluded, Dryden's original two-year contract with the Canadiens also expired. Ken had been earning a modest salary despite his enormous appeal. He believed that he deserved more money; he also was acutely aware that the rival World Hockey Associa-tion was prepared to offer him a fat contract to lure him away from the NHL.

"It was an unbelievable situation," he reflects. "Agents were coming out of the woodwork everywhere, and some of them weren't particularly reputable. They made promises with no solid footing."

Dryden repeatedly asserted that his decision would not be based solely on dollar signs. "I would never consider dollars alone," Ken explains. "I always considered Montreal, the city, a great place. I really like it . . . and playing here for a winning team, a prestigious team in a prestigious league. I also weighed whether my future was in Canada or not. There were many things, more than dollars."

Finally, Dryden reached an agreement with Pollock and the Canadiens. He signed a new two-year contract. "I considered Dryden the top goalie in the NHL," says Pollock. "And his contract reflected that opinion."

So did Dryden's performance during the 1972–73 season. After playing capably for Team Canada in the September 1972 series with the Soviet team, Ken recorded a 2.26 goals-against average with six shutouts in 54 games, ten fewer than the year before. He won the Vezina Trophy, given to the goaltender on the team surrendering the fewest goals.

If Ken's ability remained unquestioned, his durability suffered doubts because of a back ailment that had originally bothered him the previous season and returned to put him out of action in late

January and February 1973. The sabbatical had a therapeutic effect, however, and Ken returned to the Montrealers in top shape as the Canadiens solidified their hold on first place in the East. Then, for the second time in three seasons, Dryden paced his team to the Stanley Cup, as the Habs rolled over Buffalo, Philadelphia, and Chicago.

Now it appeared that the sky was the limit for Dryden. He had reached the peak of his game and seemed a fixture at the Forum. But then Dryden dropped a bombshell. He announced that, at age 26, he was retiring from hockey. Rather than tend goal for the Canadiens, Dryden took a job "articling" for the Toronto law firm of Osler, Hoskin, and Harcourt. The job paid a trifling $7500 a year. Everyone from his teammates to his law colleagues wondered what had prompted Ken to make such a dramatic decision. When Dryden entered pro hockey, it had been known that there was a possibility of his retiring if big-league hockey prevented him from completing his law studies. But Ken already had completed his three required years of university.

However, Dryden's close friends realized that his decision had more to do with factors other than his legal career. In fact, he had been unhappy with the two-year contract he had signed the previous season. Salaries had skyrocketed because of the bidding war between the NHL and the WHA. Dryden insisted that he be paid on a par with other top players in the league. If the Canadiens would not meet his demands, he gladly would work for a meager salary to pursue his law career.

"If I was to have an ongoing relationship with the Canadiens," says Dryden, "they had to be reasonable about money. The earlier contract upset me. I felt that the relationship couldn't be maintained unless they made some changes."

The Canadiens wouldn't budge and Dryden departed. Thus, the Canadiens were left with three unproven young goaltenders—Michel "Bunny" Laroque, Wayne Thomas, and Michel Plasse. None of the three could fill Dryden's skates and, not surprisingly, the Habs were knocked out of the first playoff round by the Rangers.

Meanwhile, Ken had immersed himself in the routine of the law world. He took a small apartment in Toronto, and signed as a defenseman with a local industrial league team. In his spare time, Dryden did "color" commentary for Toronto Toros WHA hockey telecasts. Dryden had made his point; he proved to the Canadiens by sitting out the season that he was quite serious about becoming a full-time lawyer. He also observed big-league hockey from a less positive viewpoint. "I saw violence," he recalls. "I'm not sure I noticed it more as a spectator or if it was always there. Maybe as a player it occurred and I never paid much attention to it."

After considerable give-and-take Ken and the Canadiens finally came to terms. He had taken, and passed, his bar exams before signing a new three-year NHL pact.

Ken's return to major league hockey did not erase the worries of Montreal fans. Would he be the same flawless Ken Dryden after a year's absence?

The pressure hardly disturbed the large goaltender. "There'll be some adjustment," Dryden said at the time, "but just for a few games."

He was wrong. Dryden suffered several problems. He mishandled routine shots that would have been simple saves for him two years earlier. He was conspicuously weak in a home game against the Los Angeles Kings and was showered with boos. "At the time," says Dryden, "I couldn't blame them."

Dryden was handling the puck as if it was covered with household oil. "The shots themselves were no problem," he explains, "but my timing was way off. Timing is the difference between having the puck bounce off the heel of the glove or catching it in the pocket. Facing difficult situations again was a bigger problem than facing shots. When you haven't seen NHL plays developing in front of you for a year it takes time to decipher them again.

"For example, a player came across our blue line and set up a trailer to the man coming behind him. A goalie has to react a certain way. Because some plays seemed a little strange to me, I wasn't reacting instinctively. Also, there was the concentration, disciplining myself to concentrate for the complete 60 minutes. I didn't have to concentrate quite that

Ken Dryden talks to the press.

much as a defenseman in the industrial league."

Montreal rooters were distressed as Ken played poorly through October and November. As the media grew increasingly hostile, Dryden's frustration multiplied. "I was disheartened and discouraged," he recalls. "It was very difficult. I went over the goals that had been scored against me in my mind. I'd say: 'that's how I played it and it didn't work. Therefore, perhaps, there should be changes.' I questioned things and I became confused."

Worse still, Dryden became so disgusted that he blamed his own defensemen. He charged that three-quarters of the shots against him should never have reached the net.

"A good defense is extremely frustrating to the other team," he asserted. "If a team is a bit tired or hurting a bit, they might be looking for an easy time. A good defense will slow them up and if you're a couple of goals ahead, they'll realize early in the game that they're not going to catch up. They'll give up. They'll start thinking about the next game."

Canadien Coach Scotty Bowman betrayed his despair with Dryden by allowing Bunny Laroque to take over as Montreal's number one goalie as the Canadiens battled for first place with the Kings in the homestretch. But Laroque proved inadequate and Dryden returned to the nets for the final Los Angeles–Montreal confrontation. The Canadiens, at last, captured the pennant by eight points. Although Dryden's play had significantly improved, he was not credited with returning the club to its winning ways. One Toronto columnist wrote:

"Ken Dryden is back in goal, all right, after that year off. But he hasn't been personally responsible for the turnabout, as so many people assumed he would be. Indeed, Bunny Laroque has been tending the Habs' nets as well as Dryden. No, Dryden may yet become the goalie he used to be, but you have to look elsewhere for an explanation of the Canadiens' resurgence."

When all the statistics had been fed to the computer, Ken owned a respectable 2.69 goals-against average, with four shutouts to his credit. Now he was on the Stanley Cup firing line once more.

In the playoffs, the Canadiens met a low-scoring Vancouver Canucks club after receiving a bye in the preliminary round. Dryden allowed only nine goals in Montreal's quarter-final victory over Vancouver. The semifinals were conspicuously more difficult as the Canadiens faced the high-powered Buffalo Sabres led by the awesome "French Connection Line" of Gilbert Perreault, Rick Martin, and Rene Robert. In the first two games in Buffalo, Ken was strafed with 79 shots of which he stopped 69. Montreal lost both games as Dryden's supporters argued that the Canadiens' defense had let him down. Undaunted, the Habs rallied to tie the series in Montreal, but Buffalo took the fifth game in overtime at the Sabres' home rink as they bombed Dryden with 45 shots. The Canadiens were dispatched from the playoffs in the sixth game at the

Ken Dryden follows the puck.

Forum. Dryden's goals-against average for the series was 3.50, but the effervescent Sabres averaged 30.5 shots a game.

Was it Dryden's fault that Montreal failed? Only to the extent that he had not found his form after the one-year layoff. In 1975–76, he was as sharp as he had been in his halcyon years, and the Canadiens dominated the NHL, finishing with the highest regular season point total in history. They won the Stanley Cup, and Dryden saw his goals-against average drop to 2.03 with a league-leading eight shutouts, and the Canadiens won the Vezina Trophy.

Dryden continued his fine play in the playoffs, as the Canadiens swept to the Stanley Cup in 13 games. Ken recorded a goals-against average of 1.92.

But there was bad news with the good. Dryden had felt a twinge in his knee during the final playoff game of 1976. The twinges continued to plague him and then the knee locked, a warning signal of cartilage trouble. Surgery was performed and Dryden was compelled to miss the Canada Cup series preceding the 1976–77 season.

Ken was uneasy during training camp. "You have to regain confidence after surgery," Dryden explains, "and become convinced it will respond to any circumstances. You gain that confidence by being in playing situations and that's what we have to wait for."

Dryden showed little effects of the injury during the season. Playing in 56 games, he had a goals-against average of 2.14, with ten shutouts. And it was the same story in the playoffs, as the Canadiens again captured the Cup easily.

The 1977–78 season ended with Dryden accumulating a tidy 2.05 goals-against average—the best of any netminder.

By this time, Dryden had experienced enough excitement for an entire career—Stanley Cups, Vezina Trophies, a Conn Smythe Trophy, a retirement and a superlative comeback. Better still, Dryden, in his low thirties, is approaching his prime. Unless he prematurely leaves hockey to pursue his law career, NHL shooters can look forward to several reasons of vainly seeking an opening to put the puck behind this cultural, charismatic goal-tending Goliath.

53

GUY LAFLEUR

Translated from the French, Lafleur means "the flower." In the case of Montreal Canadiens' Guy Lafleur, the flower required more time than expected to bloom. After three pro seasons of anxiety and disappointment, the lyrical French-Canadian blossomed like an American beauty rose. Within four seasons, (1974–75, 1975–76, 1976–77, 1977–78) Guy scored 225 goals and the Canadiens were kings of the rink.

Lafleur can pirouette on the ice as Rudolph Nureyev can on the stage. Lafleur is graceful to a fault. With liquid grace, he seems to flow effortlessly around and between the enemy lines. A hopeful opponent lining him up for a bodycheck often collides with thin air as Lafleur zigzags out of danger, detecting oncoming bodies with his special ice radar. Then, he motors away with a burst of speed or a cute sidestep. In the offensive zone Guy controls the puck for long periods, darting behind the net, and then back out, awaiting an opening to unleash his lethal shot or precision pass. Although he stands six feet, 175 pounds, Lafleur nevertheless appears frail, but he seldom is muscled out of a play and has experienced only one major injury—a broken finger after being slashed by Toronto's Darryl Sittler.

Lafleur's extravagant accomplishments could not have been forecast when he was a frail lad growing up in the pulp mill town of Thurso (pop. 4000) Quebec. It was Guy's good fortune that his father was a positive influence on him early in life.

"My father, who was a welder," says Guy, "took me out to play hockey for the first time when I was four years old. And from then on I just seemed to take to the game."

Petite Guy steadily climbed the rungs of Thurso's town leagues from bantam to midget, squeezing in school work as well.

"Guy was always more interested in hockey than in school," recalls his father. "Though he always got through. He used to sneak into the arena and play by himself until the manager discovered him and realized he was good. After that he could play anytime."

Guy attracted the attention of scouts when his team travelled to the metropolis of Quebec City to participate in the playoffs. Particularly interested were the Quebec (Junior) Aces (later the Quebec Remparts) of the Quebec Amateur Hockey Association. They knew a jewel when they saw one.

When Guy was 14, he received an invitation to play for the Quebec team, but Lafleur's father believed that his son was too young to go to Quebec City and live with a strange family. But in 1966, the following year, Guy's dad consented to the move.

Lafleur's season away from home both on and off the ice was disastrous. He played in only eight games, scoring once. Between games, he was often

Guy Lafleur scores against St. Louis.

lonely, as one might expect of a teenager in foreign surroundings.

"The first year was the worst," Guy remembers. "I was only 15, and most of my teammates were 18 and 19. I was too young to go out with them, and I didn't know many other people in the city. It was pretty terrible at times."

Guy's fortunes improved the following year as he scored 30 goals; he followed that up with a 50-goal season, suggesting that the scouts' appraisal of Lafleur was correct.

But it was in the 1969–70 season, his fourth year with the Remparts, that the name Lafleur became a household word in Canada. Guy scored an unprecedented 103 goals. More importantly, Lafleur was impressive in other areas of the game.

"He never stops," says Maurice Filion, who was Guy's coach with the Remparts. "He's a worker. He's not only a scorer, but he backchecks, he plays defensively, he can dig the puck out of a corner, he can get it to the net, he can shift either way. And he won't be easily pushed into fights, either. It only happened twice one year, and when it did, the fights lasted one punch. That's all he takes. He's as strong as an ox."

Lafleur endured a ritual before each game in Quebec City. He would arrive at the arena five hours before the opening face-off. "I like to sit in the Coliseum by myself and think about the game," Guy says. "I play over in my mind what I think the game will be like, and I always see myself scoring between three and six goals."

On the wall near his locker room Lafleur had pasted a picture of his idol, Jean Beliveau, then captain of the Montreal Canadiens. Beliveau's career was winding down, so where else would a French-Canadian lad with many of Beliveau's skills ultimately land but in the National Hockey League with the Flying Frenchmen, the Canadiens.

Lafleur still was eligible to play another year in the juniors after his 103-goal season. But, with an eye to the future, Canadiens' General Manager Sam Pollock made a deal with the struggling California Golden Seals. Pollock dealt mediocre forward Ernie Hicke and Montreal's first choice in the 1970 draft for the Seals' first pick in the 1971 draft, for which Lafleur would be eligible. The Seals used the Ca-

nadiens' pick to select Chris Oddliefson, who later starred for the Vancouver Canucks.

Meanwhile, Guy caused a revival of the Remparts, who just prior to his arrival had averaged only 1000 fans a game. The fans emerged in large numbers to see Lafleur.

Reacting to his 103-goal season, Lafleur says: "I could have done 20 goals better." So the following season, he went out and scored an astonishing 130 goals and 79 assists in only 62 junior games.

Consequently the attention of NHL fans during the 1970–71 season was focused not on the races for first place, but on the battle for last! The team finishing with the fewest points would be rewarded with Guy Lafleur as the first pick in the 1971 amateur draft. Unless, of course, that team was the Seals, in which case the rich would get richer— Lafleur would be a Montreal Canadien.

At the time the Los Angeles Kings were the chief threat to the Seals for the NHL cellar. The Canadiens' high command did not stand idly by and observe the battle. Pollock sent veteran Ralph Backstrom to the Kings to help them stay out of last. When the Minnesota North Stars drifted toward the bottom, the Canadiens sent them center Gord Labossiere as insurance. Ultimately, California finished last, and the Canadiens had their Guy.

Like any youngster growing up in Quebec, Guy was hopeful of being selected by the Canadiens. But he was ready to go anywhere. "I would even have gone to California," he says. "Although it always has seemed to me that California is the wrong climate to play hockey. For big-league hockey the climate, in my mind, has got to be cold. Anyway, there doesn't seem to be much fan spirit in California. The players are like factory workers; nobody knows them. Here, in Montreal, the players are stars."

However, Lafleur suffered some reservations about being picked by Montreal. "I wanted to get a lot of ice time," he explains, "and I was afraid Montreal would keep me on the bench or send me to the minors. I saw what Gilbert Perreault was doing for Buffalo (38 goals in his rookie year) and I wanted to get a chance to play like him."

Nevertheless, Lafleur was confident that he would make it in the NHL. "I figured I would be all right. I've played with Perreault and I thought I was as good as he was. I thought I might even be a star in Montreal because I was popular in Quebec, and people in Montreal and Quebec seem to like the same people."

Whether he knew it or not, Lafleur already was a star in Montreal without having put on a bleu, blanc et rouge (blue, white and red) uniform. Already, he was being acclaimed on Rue Ste. Catharine as the next Beliveau. A controversy erupted over whether Beliveau's number 4 should be retired or passed on to Lafleur. Guy, himself, settled the dispute.

"I never wanted number four," Guy says. "I tried to follow Beliveau, not in style and number, but in

example. I admired Bobby Orr and Gordie Howe, too, you know.

"But it didn't really matter what number I got. I knew I would be there just to play hockey. I would have enough to worry about. Besides, there were the expectations of the fans. I had done so well in the juniors and I had so much publicity that I knew there was going to be a lot of pressure on me."

Indeed there *was* a lot of pressure from Montreal's fans, who always demanded excellence and took special pride in the accomplishments of French-Canadian players. With Beliveau gone, Lafleur would have to take his place, and a 50-goal season was unrealistically expected by many.

All eyes were riveted on Lafleur during the Canadiens' training camp in September 1971. To fulfill the "Beliveau destiny," Guy was shifted to center from his regular right wing position. The transition to the NHL was supposed to be a natural step for Lafleur, as it was for Beliveau, a center, nearly 20 years earlier.

To the dismay of Montreal fans, instead of flying with his fellow Frenchmen, Guy sputtered and slumped, orbiting only occasionally for a total of 29 goals and 35 assists for 64 points. It was considerably below expectations, and even more disappointing was the fact that Buffalo Sabres' rookie Richard Martin had scored 44 goals in *his* rookie season. Still worse, Guy often lacked the dipsy-doodling moves he had used so effectively as a junior. He worried about his defensive play and seemed reluc-

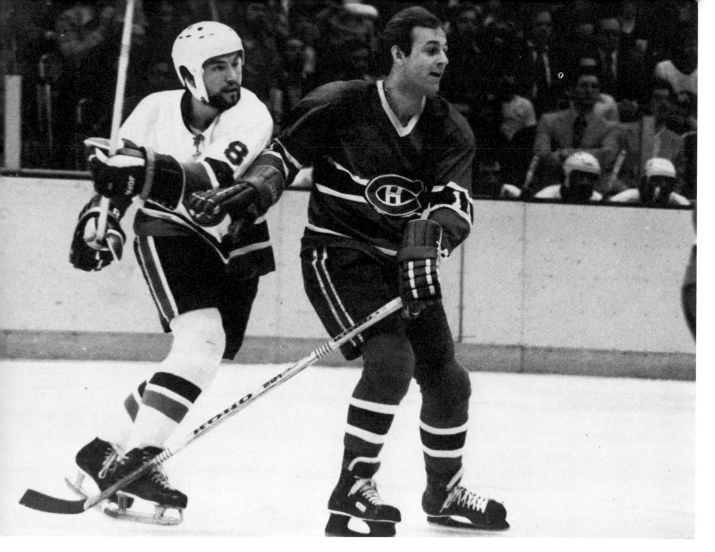

The Flower of Hockey, Guy Lafleur

tant at times to attack for fear of being caught out of position up ice. Restless, the Canadiens shifted him between center and right wing, hoping to find a solution. Adding to his woes was loneliness in French-Canada's largest city. "That first year I spent more time in Quebec than I did in Montreal," he recalls. "Every chance I got I drove back to be with my friends. I'd drive to Montreal, practice, and then drive right back to Quebec. In Montreal I had Jean Beliveau as my only friend I could talk to. I'd met him years before when I played in the peewee tournament in Quebec and he was there to open it. Beliveau was my biggest help. I always went to him. I always could talk to him. After all, he had seen it all."

Statistically, the 1972–73 season was similar to Guy's first year, as he scored 28 goals and 27 assists. But Canadiens' Coach Scotty Bowman defended his player after he scored his 50th NHL goal —more than three-quarters of a season too late according to Lafleur's critics.

"I don't know what everyone was expecting," says Bowman in retrospect. "This was the kid's second year in the NHL and he had just scored his 50th goal. There aren't many who have done so well." One meaningful change was an improvement in Lafleur's play after he was placed at center on a line with Rejean Houle and Marc Tardif. "At first he was poking in a lot of goals from scrambles around the net," Bowman explains. "But soon he began putting them in with good shots. Lafleur's got one of the quickest, hardest wrist shots in the league."

Hopeful fans waited for Guy to explode during the 1973–74 season, but his production dropped to 21 goals and 35 assists for 46 points. Astonishingly, his mentor, Beliveau, publicly blasted Lafleur. Guy had become discouraged; he was missing optional practices, and many people questioned his attitude. Beliveau's chewing-out didn't increase Lafleur's goal production that season, but it provided a long-range positive change in the youngster's attitude.

"He didn't say anything that he hadn't already said to me privately," Guy recalls, "but it was good. It awakened me. It made me think, 'Now I'm going to show that guy.' I was missing too many chances and saying, 'Oh, forget it.' I wasn't going after the puck. I'd say, 'Oh, what's the use!' I didn't have the confidence; I wasn't doing everything I could."

Despite his reconditioned attitude, Guy still skated as if two cylinders were missing.

Lafleur's Canadiens' contract expired at the end of the 1973–74 season at a time when the World Hockey Association was in full bloom. Guy's father-in-law was then a director of the WHA's Quebec Nordiques, and the club made a substantial offer to Lafleur. This time, Beliveau interceded at the eleventh hour and Lafleur came to terms with the Canadiens for an estimated $1 million.

Guy Lafleur in full flight against the Capitals

Apparently, the long-term contract provided a psychological tonic. It gave Guy a sense of security, enabling him to calm down and concentrate on hockey. The catharsis was evident when Lafleur came to the September 1974 training camp in excellent shape. That summer he had run, waterskied and played tennis.

Yet the results were two weeks in coming as Guy went scoreless for the first four games of the regular season. Then, in the fifth game, there was what Coach Scotty Bowman calls "a turning point" in Lafleur's career.

Bowman employed Lafleur as a penaltykiller for the first time in his career. "He hadn't scored a goal up to then," says Scotty, "but from that time on he really started to show a lot. Giving him the extra responsibility seemed to work wonders."

Lafleur then went scoreless again for two games, but he really broke the ice—and dented the twine—in Game Eight against the Detroit Red Wings. To railbirds, Lafleur skated like a man reborn. He went on a scoring spree in which he averaged nearly a goal a game for the next three months. He splurged with two three-goal "hat tricks," and a four-goal game against the Pittsburgh Penguins. Like a super-charged rocket, Guy propelled himself toward the top of the NHL scoring race and appeared destined for a 50-goal season. In fact, it seemed possible for him to score 60 or 65. It also meant that he had become a marked man and, in early February, Guy's hand was slashed by Toronto Maple Leafs' center Darryl Sittler. The blow broke a finger in Lafleur's left hand, putting him out of action for a month. The injury cost Guy his chance to win the scoring title. At the time Guy had 44 goals and 52 assists in 54 games (including the seven games at the beginning of the year in which he had no goals), and he trailed the Boston Bruins' Phil Esposito by only seven points.

Despite the broken finger Lafleur reached the coveted 50-goal mark. On March 29, 1975, he scored his 50th against the Kansas City Scouts (now the Colorado Rockies) at the Forum. A thunderous ovation poured down from the rafters as Montreal toasted their hero.

Guy Lafleur had finally arrived.

By season's end, he had scored 53 goals and 66 assists for 119 points, an all-time Montreal record for most points in a year. Lafleur believes he has an explanation for the turnabout.

"I was always thinking about Quebec City," he says. "People from there still wanted me to come back and play hockey for the Nordiques. But then I signed my new contract with the Canadiens and I bought a home in Vercheres, near Montreal. My wife, Lise, was expecting a child. Now I had real responsibilities."

There are other explanations for Lafleur's metamorphosis. During training camp, he surprised teammates by discarding his helmet, which he had used throughout his career. Without the protective headgear, he played with more abandon and seemed quite willing to absorb punishing body contact to make a play. In addition, he was playing on a set line at right wing, with center Peter Mahovlich and left wing Steve Shutt.

"He was no longer afraid to hang on to the puck until he could make a big play," says Coach Bowman. "That's the rarest quality in a young player. You see it in a Stan Mikita but not in many others. Guy almost always makes a play. He's half a play ahead of everyone else, sensing where the opening

Guy Lafleur scrabbles with Bryan Trottier for the puck.

will be. That anticipation is what sets the great ones apart. You can't coach it. I had doubts. Claude Ruel (assistant coach) had worked with Lafleur from the start and always said that when Guy's 25 he's going to be an accomplished, complete hockey player. Claude would tell me that when I kept asking, 'Is he going to come through?' "

Teammates also marvelled at Lafleur's transformation from pedestrian player to superstar. "When I first saw him, I thought he was an average hockey player," says linemate Steve Shutt. "Then, in Chicago during his second season, he gave us a taste of what was inside that shyness. He simply faked out the entire Black Hawks' team—skated through them like they weren't even on the ice. Our captain Henri Richard said, 'Did you see that? No one can do that.' After that we knew it was just a matter of getting that kind of play out of him all the time." When Richard retired he was succeeded by Yvan Cournoyer, who empathized with the younger Lafleur.

"For two years," says Cournoyer, "I'd been saying that if anybody was going to bust out and score a lot of goals, it wasn't going to be Yvan Cournoyer . . . it wasn't going to be Jacques Lemaire . . . it was going to be Lafleur. He's got the moves. He doesn't wait for the puck to come to him. He goes after it. I don't have his moves. I don't think anybody in the league has Lafleur's moves."

The Canadiens finished the 1974–75 season with a rush, rallying to top Los Angeles in the Norris Division race. After beating Vancouver in the first round of the playoffs, the Canadiens were eliminated by the Buffalo Sabres in a wild, six-game series. But the Canadiens, with goalie Ken Dryden back after a year's absence and the emergence of Lafleur as a superstar, had displayed marked improvement over a disappointing 1973–74 campaign. The improvement was evident a season later as the Canadiens compiled a record of 58–11–11, the best in the NHL. And it was Lafleur who led the way, terrorizing opposing defenses with 56 goals and 69 assists for 125 points.

Relaxed and confident, Guy was the leader of the NHL scoring race for most of the season. He led Philadelphia's captain Bobby Clarke by four points, prior to the last game of the season. Montreal was at Capital Centre that night to play the Washington Caps. Lafleur assisted on linemate's Steve Shutt's 44th goal of the season, and then, late in the game with the score tied, Lafleur scored to give the Canadiens a dramatic victory.

With a six-point lead over Clarke, Lafleur's scoring title seemed safe, although the Flyers were playing the defensively weak New York Rangers. Guy had returned to his hotel room when Scotty Bowman called. Lafleur remembers the episode vividly. "Scotty asked for Guy Lafleur and I said, 'He's not here,' " Guy recalls. "I thought it was somebody bothering me for tickets. Then, he said, 'It's Scotty,'

Guy Lafleur watches the puck go in against Toronto.

and I said, 'Yeah, it's me,' and then he told me he was listening to the Flyers' game and the Rangers were winning 2–0 with a minute remaining. He said it looked pretty safe, since he didn't think Clarkie would score five points in the final minute."

Clarke didn't, and Guy Lafleur was the new scoring champion of the NHL. Guy heaved a long sigh of relief betraying the pressure of the homestretch. "If I were a lot older, I don't know if I could've coped with the pressure. I'm glad it's happening now and not later.

"The thing is, when you've done a lot of scoring and it comes down to the final weeks of the season, everybody's expecting you to keep it up. They are behind you, true, but they don't realize how hard it is on a guy to sustain the pace.

"The pressure really got bad about three–four weeks before the end when everybody was talking about my chances of winning the scoring championship. Until then, I didn't think so much about it. Then, the pressure really hit me."

Lafleur went on to help his team successively eradicate St. Louis, the New York Islanders, and the Philadelphia Flyers in just 13 games to win the Stanley Cup. Lafleur's contribution was seven goals and 10 assists for 17 points. Now his problem was coping with success. Would it spoil him? Apparently not. Lafleur started precisely where he left off during the 1976–77 season and finished with 56 goals and 80 assists, many of those to Shutt, who also cracked the 50-goal mark. Lafleur's 136 points was enough to give him an easy scoring championship. Guy's closest competitor, Marcel Dionne, finished 14 points behind.

Thus, Lafleur became only the second Montrealer ever to win back-to-back scoring titles and the only Montrealer to win the title three times. Not surprisingly, Guy also led all scorers in the playoffs, as the Canadiens won their second straight Stanley Cup, this time in only 14 games. Lafleur scored nine goals and 17 assists for 26 points.

In 1977–78 Lafleur won the scoring title for the third straight year, this time with 132 points, ahead of the New York Islanders' Bryan Trottier who had 123. Lafleur scored 60 goals—14 more than Trottier and more than anyone else in the league.

At age 26, Lafleur has conquered the hockey world. He is, as hoped, the worthy successor to Jean Beliveau.

The Flower is in full bloom.

BRAD PARK

Brad Park knows how it feels to be number two; the perennial runner-up. For nearly a decade the Toronto-born defenseman generally was regarded as the *second* best backliner in the National Hockey League—behind superstar Bobby Orr. It is a fact of life that Brad learned to live with early in his big-league career.

"I saw no reason to be upset because I was rated second to Bobby Orr," Brad says. "After all, Orr not only was the top defenseman in the game but he was considered the best player *ever* to put on a pair of skates. There was nothing insulting about being rated Number Two to such a super superstar."

Although Orr, even in retirement is regarded as the supreme hockey player, Brad proved to be as important to the New York Rangers, with whom he broke into the big leagues, as Orr was to the Boston Bruins. It is ironic that since Orr left the Bruins, Brad Park has become the top skater in the Hub.

Now, as the Bruins' leader, Park along with Denis Potvin and Larry Robinson is—at the very least—one of the best defenseman in the world and is not rated below anyone.

Park's image, however, is deceptive. His baby face suggests a choirboy, not a crushing hockey player. But on the ice, Park excels in every phase of the game including brutal hip checks, one of his more destructive trademarks. Brad also is adept at choreographing the attack out of his own end of the rink with fancy rushes and clever passes. Offensively, Park owns one of the most accurate and speedy slapshots, which he distills with uncanny playmaking ability. This defensive artistry is rooted in a past that always was dominated by nets and skates.

Park started toying seriously with a stick and puck when he was six. His brother Ron, two years older, already was playing organized hockey. Ron's presence on the rink provided the ideal motivation for Brad.

"He couldn't see why he couldn't play if his older brother already was in the game," says Mrs. Park. "Brad bugged his dad until, finally, he let him play goal. When he found out Brad actually could skate he put him up front and let him try for goals."

At age seven, Brad entered a league in the Scarborough area of Toronto, and was named assistant captain of a club called the Eglinton Aces. Young Park's performances were enough to win a promotion to the Peewee division, where Brad played on a team coached by his father.

"Playing on a team my father coached wasn't easy," Brad recalls. "Once, we won a game, 6–0, and he came into the dressing room and blasted us. 'You guys got a shutout,' he said, 'but you made mistakes left and right.'" Tough as the criticism may have been, it did help and as the years unfolded Brad's dad had a positive effect on his

Brad Park of the Boston Bruins

hockey career. Besides coaching him as a young-ster, Bob Park advised Brad about contract negotiations, and often phoned Brad with constructive criticism after games during his rookie season in the NHL.

Brad's mother Betty also freely dispensed advice to her hockey-playing son. "I was critical of him," Betty Park admits. "If he didn't throw a good body-check within the first few minutes that he was on the ice, I felt he wouldn't play the kind of game he was capable of playing. Bob and I have always felt that constructive criticism is helpful. When he was young, Brad always needed an incentive."

When Bob Park's job was transferred to Montreal, the family moved there. Brad, then 15, skated for a Montreal Junior B team. After six months in the Quebec metropolis, Bob Park was transferred back to Toronto, where he was asked to coach the Neil MacNeil High School Junior B team, an affiliate of the Toronto Marlboros. The Marlboros were associated with the Toronto Maple Leafs of the National Hockey League. Bob wanted to see Brad play with the hometown Leafs, and he kept the NHL team officers up-to-date on his son's progress in amateur hockey.

The Neil MacNeil team folded after Brad had been with the club for one season. Park was then invited to try out for the Marlboros, at that time one of Canada's most prestigious amateur teams. Brad knew that dozens of Marlboro graduates had moved successfully up to the NHL, and that he too now had a shot at the top.

After an intensive tryout at the Marlboros' audition, Brad was informed that he had made the Marlboros A club in his first try. He would be the fifth defenseman.

His joy was fully justified but was soon dampened by the first of a chain of serious injuries that has hampered him throughout his amateur and professional career. During his second season with the Marlboros, Brad played despite a swollen eye suffered in a fight with (future teammate) Don Luce. With his vision impaired, he found it difficult to sight the enemy and was nailed by a hard check delivered by another future teammate, Sheldon Kannegeisser. The result was some substantial ligament and cartilage damage to his right knee. Having recovered from that blow, Brad took a severe jolt to his kidneys that put him in the hospital for five weeks.

The NHL Leafs were acutely aware of the injuries and, in 1966, the Toronto sextet passed up a chance to sign Park. He thus was eligible to be selected in the amateur draft. Despite his injury record, Park was the second player selected in the draft, picked by the New York Rangers. The New York club's decision was ignored by press and fans alike as Park completed his junior career. But after the 1967–68 season, Rangers' Coach and General Manager Emile Francis took the gamble and signed

Brad to an NHL contract in May 1968. Originally, Brad had wanted more money than Francis was prepared to offer, but Bob Park stepped in with some fatherly advice. Bob looked his son straight in the eye and said: "First, Brad, you have to prove yourself in the majors before you make any outsized demands. If you can do that, then you can come back here and tell Mr. Francis what you think you're worth. But not a minute sooner!"

Park signed a two-year contract with the Rangers for a then modest $28,000. Now it was a matter of proving to his father, his manager and, most of all, himself that he was fit for the big time.

In September 1968, Brad arrived at the Rangers' training camp in Kitchener, Ontario, as one of three young defensemen hoping to win a place on the varsity. The others, with better credentials at the time, were Mike Robitaille and Al Hamilton. The latter was given the best chance of making the team mostly because the Rangers had had their eyes on Hamilton for several years and believed he was mature enough for the majors.

Though Brad was well aware that he was given scant hope of becoming a full-time Ranger defenseman, he remained totally optimistic.

"I came to the camp not expecting to be a fringe defenseman," Brad recalls. "I figured I could knock off the third or fourth regular defenseman. That way I wouldn't have to worry about being fifth. I genuinely felt I could make the club."

Hamilton and Robitaille were competent but lacked Brad's bubbly desire. Besides, one thing Park had going for him was an overwhelming urge to throw bodychecks—a quality the Rangers craved at the time. With his dad watching happily in the stands, Brad hit everyone in sight. This was rather appropriate since his father was largely responsible for Brad's expertise in the art of bodychecking, specifically the perfectly synchronized hip check.

"My father had always insisted that I engage in a lot of body contact," Park remembers, "and learn to take an opponent out of the play. This wasn't easy when I was very young because I was one of the shortest players around. I didn't reach five feet until I was 14 years old. I couldn't knock down the big fellows, so I'd fall in front of them."

The battle for the varsity between Park, Hamilton, and Robitaille went down to the wire and despite his superb showing, Park was dispatched to Buffalo of the American League while Hamilton was retained as the Rangers' fifth defenseman. Many objective critics believed that the Rangers had picked the wrong man.

"We've been promising Hamilton a chance," Francis explained to Park. "He deserves one good shot at it, and we don't want you just sitting on the bench where you won't get any experience. In Buffalo you'll get lots of ice time and you'll improve. If we call anybody up from Buffalo, you'll be the first!" Time would prove Francis true to his

Brad Park hustling back on defense

word. Hamilton was given his chance, but he failed to produce. Meanwhile, at Buffalo, Park played in 17 games and scored two goals and 12 assists. More than that, Brad had quickly become a major presence on the ice, asserting himself physically, with 49 penalty minutes.

In early December 1968, Al Hamilton was demoted to Buffalo while Park was brought to Broadway. At first Brad played well, but soon was benched by Coach Bernie Geoffrion when the team plummeted into a horrendous slump at Christmas. But in January 1969, Francis, who previously had given up coaching before the season's opener to concentrate on his job as general manager, returned behind the bench. Where Geoffrion had denied Brad ice time, Francis gave him an extra workload. The rookie responded by playing hard-hitting defense, and, although he was not scoring goals, Park soon was setting up scores with his crisp radarlike passes.

It was all peaches-and-cream until late in the season when Brad received his official "welcome" into the rough and tumble of big-league hockey. New York was at Olympia Stadium in Detroit facing the Red Wings. The artistic but vicious Gordie Howe attempted to elude Brad's menacing hip in the Rangers' zone. Nevertheless, Brad devastated Howe with a well-timed low check. "I was told to go low on the man," Brad recalls, "because if I went high

Gordie might give me a hunk of stick in the mouth. That I didn't need."

Having disposed momentarily of Howe, Brad swerved up ice, failing to keep an eye on Howe in his rearview mirror. Meanwhile, Howe regained his feet and pursued Park. The wily veteran overtook the naive, unsuspecting rookie, raised his stick and caught Park square in the neck, knocking him colder than a supermarket herring.

Rangers' trainer Frank Paice rushed onto the ice and revived Brad with the help of smelling salts. When Park had finally pulled himself together he skated directly at Howe, pointed a finger in a High Noon confrontation and warned: "One more like that, and this stick goes down *your* throat!" The warning, solemn though it was, did not frighten Howe, but it earned Park the respect he craved from the Red Wing ace. That was most important and soon word of such incidents spread quickly through the NHL; Brad had established himself as an athlete to be treated with respect, despite his youth. The respect grew as Park's performances continued to sparkle and, inevitably, he began to invite comparisons to the gifted defenseman Bobby Orr. The conclusion was that although Brad truly was exceptional he was no Bobby Orr.

Brad originally had obtained his first look at Orr at Toronto's Maple Leaf Gardens when Orr skated for the Oshawa Generals; Brad was then a member of the Marlboros. Orr went around Park as if Brad was a totem pole and set up a goal. It was an embarrassing episode but one that had a therapeutic effect on Brad. Instead of becoming jealous of Orr, Park chose to learn from him. "Bobby has had a definite influence on my play," says Park. "I guess he's influenced most young defensemen. I began watching and studying him right away during my rookie year. I knew he did things I couldn't do and I wasn't about to copy him. What influenced me most was the general way he operated on the ice."

Ironically, Brad scored his first NHL goal against Bobby Orr & Company, during a rout of the Bruins at Madison Square Garden. The year was 1969. The red light marked the first of three goals and 23 assists for 26 points in 54 big-league games. The Rangers finished third but were then eliminated in four straight Stanley Cup playoff games by the Montreal Canadiens, as Brad picked up two more assists.

Hopes were high for both Brad and the Rangers when the curtain lifted on the 1969–70 season. New York had an abundance of talent and, in Park, a leader on the ice, even if just a 21-year-old second-year man. The Rangers, as anticipated, played well from the start, and moved to the top of their division. Park, in turn, made the All-Star team, and was looking more and more like Bobby Orr every day. Park's quality performance in the All-Star classic, despite his suffering with 102° fever, drew critical raves. At times during the game, Park was paired with Bobby Orr, for what hockey fans regarded as a dream team. Little did any onlookers believe that the day would ever come when Park and Orr would be on the Boston Bruins together.

Everything was hunky-dory for Brad until the night of February 19, 1970, when the Rangers again visited Detroit. New York was hugging first place at the time and the brilliant play of Park was a main reason why. But, as has so often befallen the New Yorkers, who have not won the Stanley Cup since 1940, bad luck struck down the prodigy.

It happened as Brad pursued a loose puck in the corner along with Detroit defenseman Carl Brewer. As the irresistible force met the immovable object, Brewer crashed down on Park's ankle. Brad was rushed to the hospital where X rays revealed a broken ankle. Doctors informed Brad he would be out for the remainder of the season.

Without Park in the lineup, the Rangers disintegrated. Not only did they drop out of contention for first place, which they had occupied for weeks, but in little more than a month they were in danger of missing the playoffs completely.

Despite medical warnings, Park returned near the end of the season in a desperate attempt to revive the team. His gallant comeback helped the New Yorkers to gain a playoff berth, although the Rangers were once again eliminated in the first round.

This time the term "genius" worked for Brad who was elected as a First Team All-Star defenseman, along with—of course—Bobby Orr. Brad's 134 votes placed him second only to Orr's 180. Likewise, Brad finished runner-up to Orr in the voting for the James Norris Memorial Trophy, awarded to the league's best defenseman.

"I didn't mind being Number Two," Brad still insists. "Orr gave me a challenge. If I thought the guy was better than me, I had to try harder. So I worked harder, and played better than anybody—except Orr."

Park's original NHL contract expired after the 1969–70 season. Brad implicitly believed that he had proven himself an NHL star. He was an All-Star, a major favorite of the Garden crowd, and obviously invaluable to the Rangers' success, a fact that was underlined as the Blueshirts collapsed when he was sidelined.

Yet, Francis offered Park just $17,500 for his new contract and, with the support of his father, Brad decided to hold out for more money. Francis remained stubborn and would not give in. Finally, Park was suspended from the club during training camp. The impasse appeared permanent until, after missing the team's regular season opener, Brad came to terms with Francis, signing for an estimated $30,000, plus bonuses.

"The holdout," says Brad, "was a matter of pride. Why should I have signed a contract for less

Defenseman Brad Park outflanks his foe.

than I felt I was worth?" Francis and his prideful ace eventually hammered out a pact and Brad was anticipating a banner season in 1970–71; however, it proved more frustrating for Park than satisfying. The same held true for the Rangers. Once again picked by many experts as the team to beat, New York challenged for first, but wilted in the home-stretch and settled for second behind the loathed Bruins. Park played in 60 games, ignoring a variety of injuries that would have hospitalized less doughty athletes. The most serious accident was a knee injury suffered in collision with Vancouver's behemoth defenseman Pat Quinn. This time Brad unavoidably missed nine games, but finished the season with seven goals and 37 assists for a career high of 44 points. With Park choreographing the club, his Rangers finally got by the quarterfinal playoff round, defeating the Toronto Maple Leafs in six games, but were eliminated in a memorable seven game semifinal series—including three sudden-death overtime games—by the Chicago Black Hawks.

By now it was clear to all objective observers that if Brad remained healthy he would be the best "Number Two" in the NHL and, sure enough, the following season Park stayed healthy, missing only three games, and enjoyed a spectacular campaign, with a career high of 24 goals and 49 assists for 73 points. Meanwhile, Brad's endless battle with the rival Bruins continued to escalate. Apart from Park's attempt to help his team's quest for a championship, he became embroiled in a personal battle with Boston.

In Brad's book *Play the Man*, published that year, he scathed the Bruins and their violent play with scorching prose. Park described the team as "bloodthirsty animals" at home. He did the unthinkable, candidly taking verbal potshots at individual players as well. He singled out Johnny McKenzie for his "bush" style, and added that Bobby Orr occasionally took "cheap shots" at the foe. Inevitably the Boston Bruins counterattacked in the press and in the rink. Three times during the 1971–72 season Park fought with fists and arms against them. One of his most intense confrontations was against Ted Green, about whom Park had written: "It's people like Green who give hockey a bad name." Brad won the bout although Green stunned the Ranger by butting Park in the head with his helmet.

This rivalry reached its apex in 1972 when New York advanced past Montreal and Chicago to reach the Stanley Cup finals. Their opponents were none other than the big, bad Bruins themselves. Not surprisingly, the Bruins were angry, and Brad was the recipient (and frequently deliverer) of brutal body checks. It was a classic "hate" series ultimately won by Boston in six games. Some critics felt Park had unwittingly contributed to his team's demise by firing up the Bruins with *Play the Man*. At least that was what Boston believed. "We got a lot of mileage out of that book," recalls Tom Johnson, then the Bruins' coach, now their assistant manager.

Since then, Brad often has been asked about *Play the Man* and its effect on the Rangers.

"It was honest," Park says about the book, "and I said what I had to say. I knew the Bruins would be unhappy but, frankly, I didn't think it would be as bad as it turned out."

Park's boss, Emile Francis, also was unhappy, but for different reasons. It was contract negotiation time again, only this time the World Hockey Association had been born and was throwing big money around. Already, several NHL players had shocked the hockey world by jumping leagues. The Rangers, in particular, were a target of Cleveland Crusaders' owner Nick Mileti, who offered huge contracts to several New Yorkers. Fighting money with money, the Rangers' management opened their vault to keep Brad, who received a five-year contract for an estimated $200,000 per year, the most ever paid a hockey player at the time.

Critics accused New York of "buying" a championship, but they obviously were wrong as the Rangers disappointed again, finishing third. The letdown could be traced to Park's injury early in the season when he hurt his knee after taking a hard check from Philadelphia Flyers' defenseman Ed Van Impe. Brad missed several weeks of play, and appeared in only 52 games. Still, he managed to score 10 goals and 43 assists for 53 points. Hopes for a Stanley Cup championship were buoyed after a glorious five-game upset of the defending champion Bruins, but the Rangers flattened out, losing to Chicago after winning the first game in the Windy City.

"We played well enough," Park says in retrospect, "but the puck bounced wrong and the breaks were bad. I remember when it all ended for us, I looked across the dressing room at Emile Francis and I thought he had done such a great job for the team and I felt that we had let him down. I felt like Humpty Dumpty after his fall."

For a pleasant change, Brad remained healthy during the 1973–74 season, although he was plagued by personal problems. His son, Robbie, had been born two months prematurely, and two months later the infant was in critical condition, having developed viral pneumonia. Park's older son, Jamie, also took sick. Nevertheless, Park never missed a game, and scored 25 goals and 57 assists for a team-leading 82 points.

For Brad, the ordeal with his sons ended happily —both Robbie and Jamie recovered. But for the Rangers, it was just another in an endless sequence of frustrating seasons. New York finished in third place, and were eliminated in the semifinal playoff round by the eventual 1974 Stanley Cup winners, the Philadelphia Flyers.

The loss to Philadelphia was the most humiliating of Brad's career, because his Rangers earned the dubious distinction of becoming the first established NHL team to lose a playoff series to an expansion club. Moreover, the Rangers appeared to be physically intimidated during the four games in Philadelphia's Spectrum. In the seventh game the Blue Shirts were especially timid as Dave Schultz of the Flyers pummeled Brad's big teammate Dale Rolfe.

Although it wasn't obvious at the time, New

Brad Park awaits a pass.

York's elimination by the Flyers marked the beginning of the end of the Rangers as playoff contenders —and the beginning of the end of Park's glittering career as a New Yorker. At first neither sign was clear. In fact, Francis made it seem as if Park would be a permanent Broadway fixture when Brad was named captain of the team before the 1974–75 season, replacing traded Vic Hadfield. But the injury jinx struck again. This time Brad missed six weeks because of another knee injury as a result of a collision with the Toronto Maple Leafs' Dave Williams.

On the arithmetic side, Park managed 13 goals and 44 assists in 65 games. First place, once thought possible, became elusive by mid-season. The Rangers made a run at top-rung Philadelphia in February, but then faded and barely managed to secure third place on the final weekend. The brief joy was erased in the preliminary round of the playoffs by the New York Islanders, who upset the Rangers, two games to one. Brad, ignominiously, was on the ice for the Islanders' clinching goal in the third game.

As the 1975–76 season began, Park no longer owned the Madison Square Garden fans' unequivocal affection. He was mauled with boos everytime he touched the puck. That was understandable but he also appeared to have been slowed by his injuries and, even worse, excess weight. Park no longer displayed the "joie de vivre" that had made him a favorite among the faithful; he seemed sluggish in comparison to the energetic Denis Potvin of the Islanders. Potvin was bumping Park as a superstar defenseman.

As the new season started Park and the Rangers went from bad to worse, amidst shakeups of veteran personnel that included the sale of Eddie Giacomin, once Francis' favorite goaltender. Who, the fans wondered, would be next?

Then, on November 7, 1975, THE TRADE happened. In one of the most astonishing deals in the history of the sport, Park, his teammate Jean Ratelle, and Rangers' farmhand Joe Zanussi were traded to the Bruins for Phil Esposito, one of the greatest goal-scorers in NHL history, and defenseman Carol Vadnais. As Rangers' captain, Park hardly expected to be dealt to Boston, of all places.

"At first I was very upset by the trade," Brad says. "It was a terrible shock. I thought I had 'New York Rangers' tattooed on my heart. Even now I sometimes find myself signing 'New York Rangers' after my name on autographs. I had no inkling I'd be traded; in fact, I never thought I would be. The Cat (Francis) once told me he'd never trade me. I really thought I'd be on Broadway until I was 35 or 40—you know, until I retired or something."

Disenchanted with their captain and his pudgy look, Ranger fans were ecstatic over the deal. After all, New York had obtained the great Phil Esposito, who, in 1970–71, had scored a record 76 goals, plus a capable defenseman in Vadnais. Boston obtained bad-kneed, overweight Park and a 35-year-old center in Ratelle, who appeared to be washed up. Surely, the Rangers had pulled a coup on the Bruins.

Not only was Brad stunned but he was concerned about how he would be received by once-hostile Bruins' fans. Almost immediately, the previously despised Park was greeted warmly in Boston. This was the same man who called the Bruins and their fans "bloodthirsty and animals." Now he was wearing the uniform of the "Big, *Good* Bruins." Not only that, the defensive pair that hockey fans had craved—Brad Park and Bobby Orr—had become a reality. The dream duo played the points together on the power play, until Orr, sadly, was forced to the sidelines with his bad knees.

For the Rangers, Park had scored two goals and four assists in 13 games. But in Boston, Brad came alive—with a vengeance. With Orr sidelined it was Brad who became the leader on defense, breaking up enemy rushes, and advancing the Bruins from their own end of the rink as he had done so expertly in his better years with New York.

What had inspired this metamorphosis? There were several theories. Several analysts credited Bruins' coach Don Cherry, who urged Brad to limit his offensive rushes and concentrate more on defense. Still, Park scored 16 goals and 37 assists for 53 points in just 43 games as a Bruin before his bad

knee flared up, requiring surgery. This time he missed the last 21 games of the season.

Meanwhile, the Bruins had been transformed from a mediocre team at the start of the season to serious playoff contenders. Park and the equally revived Ratelle, who himself scored 31 goals and 59 assists for 90 points, led the Bruins to bigger and better things. In the playoffs, with Park back in uniform although not at full speed, the Bruins beat a stubborn Los Angeles Kings team in seven games before being swept by the Flyers in the semifinal round.

By contrast, the Rangers floundered in last place for the entire season, missing the playoffs for the first time since the 1966–67 season.

During the 1976–77 season, Park played the most effective hockey of his career, and the Bruins, in turn, won the Adams Division race, finishing with the third best record in the NHL. Brad scored 12 goals and 55 assists for 67 points. The oft-injured Bobby Orr had gone to Chicago, and now Brad Park was *the* main man for Boston. He proved the point by pacing the Bruins all the way to the Stanley Cup finals.

The brilliant glow Brad cast over Boston Garden beamed even brighter during the 1977–78 season. Park not only skated with the authority of an All-Star, but appeared to have matured still more in his efforts to keep Boston at the top of the NHL's Adams Division. His coach Don Cherry was suitably impressed. "There isn't a defenseman in the entire league who makes a bigger contribution to his team than Park," says Cherry.

The blueprint designed by Cherry called for Park to accomplish more for the Bruins by doing less work. The coach insisted that his defenseman rush the puck less and discipline himself more than he had in the past. "The things the club wanted to accomplish in '77–'78 dictated changes in my style," Park explains. "Cherry told me he didn't want me using my energy going end-to-end on a regular shift plus working the power play and killing penalties. He said I should play a little more conservatively on regular shifts, then do the extra stuff on the specialty teams."

That the 1978 Model Park rolled smoothly was underlined by the Bruins' success. They remained among the top three teams in the NHL and the change in Brad soon became an inspiration for other coaches to revise the style of their superstars. "The change in my play," Park recalls, "can be defined in mathematical terms. Instead of trying to do too much over 200 feet of ice, I am doing more in 60 feet of ice."

Ironically, at a time when Park was reaching new heights of excellence, Bobby Orr, against whom Park frequently was compared, had been forced into premature retirement because of injured knees. It was doubly ironic that Park was orchestrating a Bruin team that once was virtually owned by Orr.

Brad Park in the penalty box

"After Orr left us," says Cherry, "we became a workingman's hockey team—a lunch-pail gang."

And champions, in their blue-collar way, because of the virtuosity of Brad Park, the new Mister Bruin.

79

DENIS POTVIN

During the 1972–73 season, their first year in the National Hockey League, the New York Islanders burrowed in the subterranean depths, setting so many negative records that they deservedly were labelled the worst team in league history. Turning such a devilishly weak club into a contender seemed a Promethean task worthy of a decade's labor.

Prior to the 1973–74 season, the Islanders took a major step toward changing their ignominious image in their rise to respectability. They signed their first pick in the 1973 amateur draft—a French-Canadian defenseman named Denis Potvin. According to many experts, the husky Potvin was the latest in the long line of "next Bobby Orrs."

Of course, nobody believed that Potvin, or anyone else for that matter, could be another Orr. But if any of the youngsters compared to Orr ever was to become as good as the magnificent Bobby, Denis produced impressive credentials. By 1978, he already had established himself as one of the top defensemen in the league, and—most important—he did what Orr and Brad Park never could do; Potvin remained healthy.

Standing six feet tall, Denis is the same size as Orr, but carries more muscle. Although he lacks the grace of Orr in his prime, Denis is, at least, his equal defensively, taking opponents out of the play with jarring bodychecks, blocking shots, and coolly leading his team out of its own end. Besides possessing a blistering slapshot that makes him a constant threat from the point on power plays, Potvin owns one of the quickest, hardest wrist shots in hockey, with which to beat many a surprised goaltender.

"There's no question," says Islander Coach Al Arbour, "that Denis is one of the best defensemen in the world."

Like Orr and Park, one could say that Denis was destined for the majors at a very early age. In fact, his brother Jean helped mastermind Denis' rise to the top from childhood days in Ottawa. Denis learned to play in his backyard with help from Jean and his father, who suffered a career-ending back injury while trying out for the Detroit Red Wings in the 1940s.

"I'm sure Dad's misfortune played a part in his directing his sons toward a hockey career," Denis says. "We were the branches of the Potvin hockey tree; Dad was the trunk, the original from which we grew."

Denis matured, physically, light years ahead of his classmates, towering over youngsters his own age. He was therefore able to play hockey against older kids, often playing with Jean and his friends.

"Jean is four years older," Denis explains, "which meant that at the time I was learning to play he was one of the 'big guys.' I wasn't timid about insisting that I be allowed to play with his gang."

Although his dad encouraged Denis to concentrate on school work, Potvin discovered that he could not devote sufficient time to both school and hockey. So, despite Potvin's high IQ, he put schooling on the back-burner. Hockey was first for Denis, although his dad often warned Denis that he could suffer an injury as he had and not be able to play hockey, in which case an education would be crucial.

"When my dad talked about his accident," Denis recalls, "I always thought, Hey, that can't happen to me. It happens to other guys but not me. Consequently, I never worried about getting hurt in a game."

Undaunted, Denis concentrated on hockey as if he were wearing blinders to shield him from the real world.

By the time Denis had reached his tenth birthday, he measured a muscular 5-8, 130 pounds. He was a terror on the ice rink and the football field, where he played fullback on his high school team.

Potvin had been playing hockey for a neighborhood team, but was concerned that he wasn't getting enough ice time so he tried out for the high school varsity. The coach, who also was Potvin's history teacher, discouraged Denis from playing hockey on the grounds that Denis had a more promising future as a football player. Cutting Denis from the hockey team, the coach insisted that Potvin was "too slow" for hockey.

Denis Potvin threads a pass.

Denis Potvin of the New York Islanders

"I was shocked," Denis says, "stunned right to the core. Not only was I rejected, but I was also being dumped from a high school team that played in a very low-level league."

His ego temporarily shattered, Denis accepted an invitation to play for a team called Altavista, one of the most prestigious amateur clubs in Ottawa. Potvin realized that Altavista would be watched by scouts for the Ottawa 67's, the town's high quality junior team, for whom brother Jean played. Although he was only 13 years old, Denis was hoping for an invitation to audition with the 67's.

But autumn camp came and went, and no invitation arrived from the 67's. Then, in January 1966, the phone rang. It was a call from Ottawa 67's Coach Bill Long asking Denis to come for a tryout. For years Long owned a reputation as one of the most respected junior coaches in Canada. His proteges included such NHL veterans as Derek Sanderson and Bernie Parent.

Long asked Denis to suit up for a game against the Niagara Falls Flyers, a strong club in the Ontario Hockey Association Junior A League. Potvin was so impressive that the local newspaper predicted that 13-year-old Denis would be "the next Bobby Orr."

Denis said good-bye to Altavista and finished the season with the 67's, and Coach Long wasted no time inviting him back for the following season. Unfortunately, a cerebral conflict made the decision rather difficult.

"In many ways football was my first love," Potvin explains. "I loved the crunch of body against body and the great feel of the outdoors. There was something special about football that appealed to me. Also there was the romance of going to an American university like UCLA. I'd watch the collegiate football games on TV, hear the roar of 100,000 people in the stands, catch the spirit of the cheerleaders, and feel terribly excited. I wanted to be a part of that American sport scene even though I was French-Canadian."

At first Denis sought a formula for the ideal compromise. Since he didn't want to relinquish either hockey or football, he attempted to swing a deal so that he could play both sports full-time, but his football coach unequivocally refused the suggestion. Forced to make a choice, Denis selected hockey because of its longer season, and because he believed he could make more money by ultimately graduating to the NHL.

"I never played football again," Denis remembers, "and, to this day, I have second thoughts about the decision. I loved football and I miss it a lot."

Based on his steady improvement on the ice, Potvin made the wise move. Although forced to compete against players six or seven years his senior,

Potvin played a body-crunching, often brutal game. His aggressiveness disturbed opponents who took umbrage at the idea of being pushed around by a 14-year-old. Aware that even the older players could not intimidate him, Denis turned tougher by the season.

In competitive hockey, there is, however, a fine line between rugged and dirty play. This line often is difficult to discern, especially for an aggressive skater like Potvin. An incident during the 1969–70 season is exemplary. Denis' team, the 67's, were playing the St. Catharines Black Hawks. One of Potvin's opponents was a player named Fran McKey who persistently needled 15-year-old Denis.

"One writer," Denis recalls, "had said that McKey had 'lots of promise and a sharp needle.' He taunted me from the opening face-off, with barbs like, 'Why doncha get the coach to change yer diapers?' "

When McKey attacked one of the 67's, Denis pursued his foe and challenged him to a fight. In the ensuing brawl, McKey was thrown to the ice and suffered a broken collarbone, a fractured skull, and two black eyes.

"I was concerned about McKey," Denis says. "He was carried off the ice on a stretcher with a face the newspaper said looked like 'a bag of golf balls.' McKey returned to the ice a couple of months later. I was glad to see the guy back in uniform; some people had warned me that he might never be able to play again."

The Potvin-McKey episode did little to disturb the natural development of Denis' talents and soon he was generally acknowledged ideal professional hockey material in terms of brains, brawn and, best of all, leadership qualities.

As Denis entered his final year of junior amateur hockey with Ottawa, his name had become a household word in Canada. His face appeared on magazine covers and everyone, it seemed, was now comparing him to Bobby Orr. Barring a serious injury, a fat contract for Potvin was as inevitable as the sun rising in the East.

Potvin completed his junior career in the 1971–72 season by scoring 35 goals and 88 assists for 123 points in only 61 OHA Junior A League games. Furthermore, he shattered Bobby Orr's junior hockey scoring record, proving that, at the very least, he was more than Orr's equal in at least one department.

The demand for Denis was such that three WHA teams produced lucrative offers for him, but Denis realized that his future was in the NHL and nowhere else.

"Three WHA teams had made offers," he says, "but I was waiting to hear from the NHL, where the real money was, not to mention the prestige."

On March 5, 1973, the New York Islanders traded veteran forward Terry Crisp to the Philadelphia Flyers for Jean Potvin. There was no doubt that the other Potvin soon would follow unless an unexpected hitch developed; and it nearly did when the Montreal Canadiens attempted to negotiate a deal for Denis.

"I didn't want to be traded to Montreal," Potvin explains, "because I was afraid I'd be under tremendous pressure to be an instant superstar with the Canadiens—and I knew there was a long list of players who had cracked under the strain of having to live up to those demanding Montreal rooters. I saw what had happened to Guy Lafleur in his rookie year; how they nearly drove him crazy, wanting him to be another Jean Beliveau, and I was anxious that nothing would come of the deal."

When it was time for Islanders General Manager Bill Torrey to announce his selection at the spring draft meetings, Montreal General Manager Sam Pollock interrupted and requested a few moments to speak with Torrey.

"It appeared my worst fears were about to be confirmed," Denis (who was there) recalls. "I'd be a Montreal Canadien in a matter of minutes."

But after a half minute of conversation that seemed like forever to Denis, Pollock returned to his seat, and Torrey announced: "The New York Islanders wish to draft as their first choice—Denis Potvin," and Denis was officially reunited with brother Jean.

Whether Denis liked it or not his image as "the

Islanders' defenseman Denis Potvin battles Chicago center Jim Harrison.

new Orr" had followed him to the NHL. But Potvin wanted to make one thing perfectly clear with the New York press and fans: "I'm not Bobby Orr and I know it. You can't compare us anyway because our styles are different. I can't skate as well as Bobby, but I feel there are a couple of other things I do better—like hitting. That's a big part of my game. I just hope I can accomplish some of the things Bobby has done, but in a different way."

A significant difference between the Potvin personality and the Orr personality was immediately apparent; Potvin was not only willing, but eager to mingle with and talk to newsmen at length. "I'm in no hurry," he says. "I've always got time to talk. I have my job, writers have theirs. A professional athlete has an obligation to answer questions. Fans like to know what the players have to say."

Like it or not Denis had been thrust into the NHL limelight—a situation fraught with problems. Not only was he a 20-year-old on whom a team that had lost 60 games the previous year was pinning its hopes, but he also found himself in direct competition with a mature star defenseman right across the county line: the New York Rangers' Brad Park.

"Brad Park," Denis says, "partly because he was a Ranger and partly because he had been an All-Star, and I aspired to that position, was one opponent who got me good and mad."

Considering the potential for problems, Denis

escaped unscathed until a snowy Sunday morning on December 16, 1973. Potvin overslept and missed the Islanders' team bus that departed for Philadelphia. Instead of trying to find an alternate mode of transportation, the confused rookie returned to his Long Island apartment and watched his mates on television as they lost to the Flyers, 4–0.

Not surprisingly, the press was harsh on Denis. A headline in the *New York Daily News* read: "SAD STORY BY AWOL POTVIN." Flyers' Coach Fred Shero said: "Maybe all that money and publicity went to his head."

Potvin was fined $500 by Bill Torrey, and ordered through a gruelling one-man workout by Islanders' Coach Al Arbour. The Islanders' high command hoped that their prodigy had learned his lesson.

"Missing the bus left a mark on Denis," Arbour explains. "He won't admit it, but he was a little uptight for the next few games. He was concerned about the stories and what the fans would think. He didn't want them to think he was irresponsible.

"To me, that was a good sign. He could have taken the other route, another outlook, and said the hell with the fine and the fans. But that wouldn't be Denis Potvin. He *does* care—about the way he plays hockey and about what people think. He hasn't missed a team bus since."

The incident soon was forgotten as Denis concentrated on hockey. His play alternated from the special to the spectacular; and in February 1974, he was rewarded with a trip to the NHL All-Star game in Chicago. Interestingly, he opened the game paired on defense with his New York rival, Brad Park. Within the hour, Denis had outshone Park and, in the third period, Potvin blasted one of his lethal slap shots past goalie Tony Esposito for his first All-Star game goal.

The score provided a welcome boost to the Potvin ego. "Just being there was a thrill," he says. "Scoring a goal was something else. I sat in the dressing room before the game and looked at the faces of the established veterans. This time a year earlier, no way I thought I'd ever be a part of this."

If further evidence of Potvin's four-star performance was necessary, Scotty Bowman, who coached Denis' East squad added: "Denis was my best defenseman; he played a great game." Now many regarded Denis as superior to Park.

"Next to Orr," said Isles' Coach Al Arbour, "Denis is the best defenseman in the league. Park is another fine defenseman, but I have to give Denis an edge over Park because of what he's done to help our club. He's been a tremendous asset from the day he joined us."

Islanders' defenseman Bert Marshall had played with both Potvin and Park, and studied their respective styles. "Brad and Denis have different techniques," says Marshall. "There are times when Brad can take more chances because he feels there will be somebody there to back him up. Denis can't do that for fear of losing the puck. But I like Denis' approach to the game. He keeps insisting he doesn't want to be 'The second Bobby Orr' but the first Denis Potvin. And I tend to agree with him."

Despite Denis' heroics, the Islanders suffered through another miserable season in 1973–74. Potvin's contribution was 17 goals and a team-leading 37 assists. The goals total was a record for a rookie defenseman as was his point total of 54. In the Calder Trophy race for rookie-of-the-year, Denis edged Atlanta's Tom Lysiak and Toronto's Borje Salming. Potvin was the first defenseman to capture the award since Bobby Orr won it in 1967. For Denis, his own performance would be a tough act for him to follow in 1974–75. But if there is such a thing as the "sophomore jinx" Potvin didn't know it. Coincidentally, the Islanders improved along with Denis and by the final weeks of the season were battling for a playoff spot in the NHL's Lester Patrick Division along with the Atlanta Flames and their local rivals, the Rangers.

Because of their surplus of "name" players, New York was favored as the intercounty foes collided in the best-of-three opening Stanley Cup round. Only a total optimist gave the Islanders a chance against the playoff-hardened Rangers.

"We thought New York would be an extremely difficult opponent," recalls Denis, "with Stanley

Denis Potvin slows a Ranger.

Cup veterans like Rod Gilbert, Eddie Giacomin, and Jean Ratelle. They also had a smart coach in Emile Francis and were fairly big, with guys like Pete Stemkowski, Jerry Butler, Ted Irvine, and Park. But for some reason, they were a club that we knew could be pushed around and even intimidated, if we manhandled them in the proper way."

Potvin was right. After splitting the first two games, the Islanders took a 3–0 lead after two periods of the decisive game at Madison Square Garden. But the Rangers staged a furious third period rally, knotting the score at 3–3, and nearly winning the game in regulation time. Only the brilliance of Islanders' goalie Billy Smith kept the Rangers from advancing.

The decisive game—and the series—would be resolved in sudden-death overtime, but few witnesses could believe how it happened. Only 11 seconds into the overtime, J. P. Parise of the Islanders scored from close range, and the new kids from Nassau County had won "The Battle of New York."

Now Potvin's spunky club moved on to the quarterfinal round against the Pittsburgh Penguins. Denis and his mates still were riding the emotional high of beating the Rangers and were victims of a buildup to a letdown. Before the Isles could pull themselves together, the Penguins had won the first three games of the best-of-seven series.

"There was no reason," Denis remembers, "considering our efforts in the first three games with Pittsburgh, to think that we might enter the record books beside the storied 1942 Toronto Maple Leafs, the only team to ever come back from a 3–0 deficit."

The Islanders, even far behind, were not to be trifled with and finally struck back at the Penguins. They won games four, five, six, *and* seven to complete a miracle comeback. In the semifinals against the Philadelphia Flyers, the Islanders again rallied from three games down but Philadelphia took the seventh game, and ended the Islanders' "miracle."

For Denis, the season of upsets proved to be a personal bonanza. He was acknowledged to be the galvanic force behind the Islanders surge of power, and emerged as "Number One" among New York hockey players, taking the top spot from Brad Park. Potvin's scoring output increased to 21 goals and 55 assists for 76 points, and, he was named to the NHL's First All-Star team, along with the ubiquitous Bobby Orr.

Denis' improvement was sustained in the 1975–76 season, although the Islanders still were unable to mount a serious challenge to the Flyers for first place in the Patrick Division. On the personal level Denis continued to cope with the challenge of Bobby Orr's presence, and as the 1975–76 season came down the home stretch, Potvin closed in on the hitherto sanctified 30-goals plateau, a level that only one NHL defenseman had ever reached, and that, of course, was Bobby Orr. As the final week arrived, the Islanders were at home against the Flyers, and Denis now had 29 goals to his credit, but the schedule was rapidly exhausting itself.

In the third period, with the Islanders already leading 3–0, Denis cranked his stick back for a slapshot from the point, and blasted it past goalie Wayne Stephenson. The Nassau Coliseum fans erupted and delivered a vociferous standing cheer for Denis, who couldn't hold back tears of joy.

"The ovation went on and on," he remembers, "and I knew I was crying. What bothered me was the television and newspaper cameras trained on me; I desperately wanted to hide my head from them so I could keep the tears to myself."

Potvin finished the season with 31 goals and 67 assists for 98 points, many of them coming on the Islanders' power play, during which he played on the point along with brother Jean. Crowning the glory was the announcement that he had won the Norris trophy as the best defenseman in the NHL; better even than Orr and Park.

During the off-season Denis signed a new five-year contract for an estimated $200,000 a year and was invited to play for Team Canada in the prestigious international Canada Cup tournament preceding the 1976–77 season. The invitation was especially meaningful for Denis because it gave him a chance both to play for his country while skating on the same team as Bobby Orr.

On the debit side was the fact that Denis soon found himself immersed in a whirlpool of controversy because of a diary he had published of his experiences and thoughts during the Canada Cup series.

In the extremely candid article, Potvin asserted that although Bobby Orr had won game MVP honors three times, Denis believed that *he* should have won it twice rather than Orr.

"It's hard for me to accept that my best game was not good enough to win it," Denis wrote after Canada's 3–1 victory over the Soviet Union. "I feel I was the best player on the ice tonight because of my two assists. I'm fair and broad-minded and I look at things pretty logically, I think, but this is something I don't understand; and I don't think I ever will."

In the diary, Potvin posed the question: "Is Bobby Orr only going to have to play to be known as the best defenseman—or is he going to have to prove it?"

Potvin's candor enraged both fans and writers alike. A Montreal writer called Denis "an insufferable crybaby." Potvin was lustily booed by fans in Montreal and Toronto.

"It disappoints me to see that people take exception to honesty," he says. "I realize that I left myself open, but I was writing down my emotions, my feelings."

Compounding Denis' problem was the fact that he was having difficulty relating to his teammates.

Denis Potvin on the attack

He seemed to be physically and psychologically apart from the players, possibly because they resented his Canada Cup article and, further, because he appeared to set himself on a pedestal above his mates. Denis was the only member of the Islanders to have an apartment in New York City, and he was interested in such cultural matters as the theatre and the arts, not the usual diet of hockey players.

In his autobiography *Power on Ice*, Denis wrote, "I guess you'd have to say many of them (his teammates) just kill time between games. Many are growing, but many are not. Many are wasting their youth. Many are wasting New York City. . . . It seems a shame that many don't take advantage of it. Most don't even do the tourist things."

Denis' off-ice problems disrupted the fine flow of his play, especially during the first half of the 1976–77 season. He finally admitted that he must learn to accept his teammates for what they are; and vice versa.

"For so long I had the feeling that the team wasn't really behind me," he says. "Like I was out there playing with five other guys, but I was really by myself."

The friction eased as the season unfolded. "I learned a lot more about intra-team relationship," he recalls. "In many ways I was wrong." Denis straightened out to produce a commendable season, although not nearly as productive as other years. Still, he managed to score 25 goals and 55 assists for 80 points.

Following the Isles loss to the Montreal Canadiens in the Stanley Cup semifinals for the second consecutive time, Denis was able to look ahead after perhaps his most difficult season ever. With his troubles now behind him, Denis regained the form that earned him the distinction of being the best defenseman in the NHL. Scoring 30 goals and 64 assists for 94 points, Potvin led the Islanders to first place in the Patrick Division. Denis had, at last, fulfilled all his notices.

DARRYL SITTLER

The label "superstar" has been applied to such distinguished NHL performers as Bobby Clarke, Guy Lafleur, Denis Potvin—and in the last few years to Darryl Sittler, the 28-year-old captain of the Toronto Maple Leafs. This even though Sittler doesn't receive half as much attention as the others; in fact, *he has never been named to an official post-season All-Star team.*

Yet Sittler is as valuable to the Leafs as Clarke is to the Flyers, or Lafleur to the Canadiens. He motors at full steam at all times, at *both* ends of the ice. He is as adept a checker as he is a scorer and playmaker. An opponent who tries to move Sittler from wherever he is stationed often receives an unpleasant souvenir of the attempt.

In short, Darryl Sittler makes the Leafs go. He is, unequivocally, their leader.

Sittler apprenticed for professional hockey with the London (Ontario) Knights, a junior team for whom he established himself as one of the top young centers in the amateur ranks. He was among the most highly coveted youngsters pursued in the NHL 1970 amateur draft.

The Toronto Maple Leafs already were well-fortified at center ice, and were searching for a wing to add some scoring punch. Their choice at the time was Greg Polis. The Leafs owned the eighth pick, and they could only hope that Polis still would be

Maple Leafs' captain Darryl Sittler

available. Hope mounted in the Leafs' camp when the first six choices were Gil Perreault, Dale Tallon, Reggie Leach, Rick MacLeish, Ray Martiniuk, and Chuck Lefley. But the Pittsburgh Penguins, selecting seventh, foiled Toronto's plans by choosing Polis.

At this point, the Leafs changed their strategy and went for the best player available, regardless of position. That man was Darryl Sittler. Negotiating through his agent, Alan Eagleson, Darryl signed a lucrative three-year contract with Toronto and the fate of the franchise was changed for the better.

Maple Leaf fans expected big things from Darryl, but Sittler was stepping into a tough position. With Dave Keon, Norm Ullman, Mike Walton, and Jim Harrison providing Toronto with depth at center, the Leafs decided to fill their vacancy at left wing by shifting Sittler to the port side against the recommendations of Bep Guidolin, Darryl's coach at London.

"Bep used to tell me about what fine moves Sittler had as a center," says ex-Leaf Coach John McLellan. "He complained we were doing the boy an injustice by playing him on the wing."

Sittler seemed uncomfortable at his new position; he often was hesitant and overcautious about getting caught out of position on defense. Nevertheless he displayed flashes of the talent for which the Leafs drafted him and he always worked hard, displaying leadership qualities rare in a rookie just turned 21.

A broken wrist sidelined him for 29 games and limited his scoring to 10 goals and eight assists. He was able to return for the playoffs, and contributed his first playoff points, a goal and an assist.

Toronto tried to move Darryl back to his natural position at the start of the 1971–72 season. They experimented by transferring Jim Harrison to right wing, creating a spot for Sittler at center. But Harrison was a flop at wing, and the plan soon was abandoned.

Returned to left wing, Sittler's problems were compounded by lingering effects of the wrist injury (he was forced to wear a protective cast during game action) and he was not at his best. Playing in 74 games, Darryl recorded 15 goals and 17 assists for 32 points.

The 1972–73 season, Sittler's third full year as a pro, saw Jim Harrison sprint for the World Hockey Association gold rush, jumping to the Edmonton Oilers. This gave Sittler another opening at center. However, the Leafs had drafted center George Ferguson from the hometown Toronto Marlboros, and he was given priority for the job. Ferguson performed well during pre-season scrimmages, which meant Darryl would remain on the wing. But when Ferguson was slowed by a groin injury, Sittler was finally returned to his favorite position, centering a line for Rick Kehoe and Denis Dupere.

Almost immediately, Sittler displayed the form that once had made him junior hockey's top cen-

Maple Leafs' ace Darryl Sittler is thwarted at the goal during All-Star game.

Darryl Sittler on the attack

terman, adding offense to his tenacious play and fiery leadership. As a result his production increased to 29 goals and 48 assists for 77 points on a nonplayoff team.

"I was never comfortable as a winger," explains Sittler. "I just wanted to play and understood the team's situation, but I never was relaxed on the wing. I'd been a center all the way in junior hockey. It seemed that the line with Harrison and me on it always played against the other team's big line. On the wing, I was so worried about my checking job that I didn't try to force things offensively.

"Center is my position. I play best when I'm aggressive, making contact and going after the puck. A center is in the middle of things all the time, forechecking, working the slot, taking faceoffs, and that's what I like."

Sittler's original contract expired following the 1972–73 season, and the timing was impeccable. Coming off a year during which he finally displayed the promise of his junior days, and with the bidding war between the NHL and the rival WHA at its peak, Sittler was in the driver's seat. On the one hand there was Leafs' President Harold Ballard and on the other was the newly born (WHA) Toronto Toros and their brash owner John Bassett.

The bidding for Sittler began in the $350,000 range over three years. Though by midsummer, Alan Eagleson was talking in terms of $1 million over five years, and Bassett was ready to meet his demands. "I said immediately that he had a deal," says Bassett. "As far as we were concerned, he wasn't to go back to the Leafs and tell them what we offered. The next thing we hear is all these additional demands—a new car for Sittler every year, a new car for his wife every second year, $100,000 in legal fees for Eagleson."

Ultimately, the Toros withdrew from the contest and Sittler signed a five-year deal with the Maple Leafs for an estimated $800,000. It has been speculated that Sittler never wanted to leave the Leafs, and the extra demands submitted to the Toros simply constituted a ploy to get them out of the negotiations. If so, Sittler and Eagleson succeeded.

"It wasn't an easy decision to make," recalls Sittler, "but the truth is I really didn't want to leave the Leafs. I knew I'd be happy with them and I wanted to stay. Signing a five-year contract looked like good business. Hockey salaries may not continue to be as high as they are right now."

The pact made Sittler the highest-paid Leaf in history, and now the pressure was on him to produce—and produce he did. Darryl continued to increase his scoring production, and further enhanced his position as the Leafs' spiritual leader. In 1973–74, he tallied 38 goals and 46 assists for 84 points, by far the highest total on the squad. More important, Sittler helped lead the Leafs out of the doldrums, as the club made the playoffs with a fine won–lost record of 35–27–16. However, Toronto drew the first-place Boston Bruins in the opening round, and bowed in four hard-fought games, with Sittler contributing two goals and an assist.

The 1974–75 campaign saw Sittler off to a bad start. His slump lasted for a month but he broke out of it in style, scoring a hat trick against Minnesota. However, the Leafs did not break out with him. Virtually assured of a playoff spot in the new NHL alignment (the Leafs were placed in a four team division, with the fourth team being the hapless California Seals) Toronto coasted to a mediocre 31–33–16 record. Although he missed eight games with an injury, Sittler scored 36 goals and 44 assists for 80 points. After getting by the Los Angeles Kings in a bitterly contested preliminary series, the Leafs were beaten in four games by the eventual champion Philadelphia Flyers in the Stanley Cup quarterfinal round.

Toronto's fiery president, Harold Ballard, decided that it was time for changes. He began his sweep-up by getting rid of two longtime Leafs, Norm Ullman and Captain Dave Keon. This meant naming a new captain and, to the surprise of no one, Ballard's choice was Darryl Sittler.

The astonishing development occurred less than half an hour after his appointment when Sittler lashed out at Ballard, the same man who had just given him the distinguished "C" as captain.

"I thought the Keon and Ullman situations were handled very badly," Sittler beefed to the media. "I know Mr. Ballard is noted for being outspoken, but in this case he was dead wrong. I don't think it was necessary to come out and say publicly that the Leafs had no further use for Dave Keon and Norm Ullman and were getting rid of them because they were washed up."

Nevertheless, Sittler was honored by the selection and welcomed his new responsibilities. "It's no secret there's been poor communication between (then coach) Red Kelly and most of the players the last two seasons," he explained. "As captain, I can do something about that."

Sittler's leadership qualities as captain reached their peak, both on and off the ice. "Darryl's not afraid to tell Ballard to go to hell," said a teammate. "Ballard's blasts hurt individual players privately but because of Sittler's attitude and counselling, we're able, as a team, to turn them into a joke."

However, the Leafs' new captain was not immune from Ballard's barbs. In February 1976, with Sittler battling a slump, Ballard was quoted as saying that he was "determined to find a sensational center" for Lanny McDonald and Errol Thompson, Darryl's regular wingers.

Sittler responded not with words, but with goals —*six of them*—and four assists, as well, in a game against the Boston Bruins the very next day. This ten-point performance, achieved at Maple Leaf Gardens against Boston goalie Dave Reece, remains an all-time NHL record, breaking the previous

The leader of the Leafs, center
Darryl Sittler

Toronto's Darryl Sittler scores against the Red Wings.

mark of eight, held jointly by Bert Olmstead and Maurice Richard of the Montreal Canadiens.

"Undoubtedly, Mr. Ballard will figure his little blast inspired me to set the record but it just isn't that way," Sittler noted.

Darryl went on to enjoy his finest season, scoring 41 goals and 59 assists to reach the 100-point mark, shattering the club's single season record of 85. The Leafs again settled for a third-place finish in the Adams Division, improving slightly on the 1974–75 year. But, still, Toronto fans called on their club for more this time as the Leafs moved past the preliminary playoff round, only to run into the Flyers in the quarterfinals for the second year in a row. However, after dropping the first two games in Philadelphia, the Leafs bounced back to tie the series at home. After the Flyers took the fifth game, the Leafs came home once again.

It was time for the captain to take over, and Sittler delivered one of the most brilliant individual performances in playoff history. His five goals led the Leafs to an 8–5 win, and forced a deciding game in Philadelphia, which the Flyers won 7–3.

Just four months later, Sittler reported to the star-studded training camp of Team Canada in preparation for the 1976 Canada Cup series preceding the 1976–77 season. And on September 15, Darryl made headlines for a third time in 1976, by scoring the winning sudden-death overtime goal in the championship game against Czechoslovakia.

"How do you explain one guy having a year like I've had?" asked Sittler in the delirious post-game locker room. "The big nights just came my way for some reason. They've all been incredible, all big thrills, but there was something pretty special about this one, scoring a goal that won a world championship for a team representing your country. Not much could top that, could it?"

Following his Canada Cup heroics, Darryl scored 38 goals and 52 assists for 90 points in 73 games. Again the Leafs settled for a third place finish with a 33–32–15 won–loss mark. Then, in a routine becoming tiring and frustrating to both the Leafs and their fans, Toronto bowed to the Flyers in seven games after surviving a three-game preliminary series, only this time they did it by blowing two games at home after stunning the Flyers with two opening wins in Philly. Sittler personally accounted for 21 of the Leafs' 31 playoff goals with his 5 goals and 16 assists. He finished the 1977–78 season right behind Guy Lafleur and Bryan Trottier in the scoring race, with 45 goals and 72 assists for 117 points. Clearly, he is Toronto's Captain Courageous, one who is destined, someday, to personally deliver the Stanley Cup to Harold Ballard.

INDEX

STAN FISCHLER, author of *Kings of the Rink*, is North America's leading hockey scribe, having written forty-five books on the subject. His column, "Speaking Out on Hockey," appears weekly in *The Sporting News* and he is coeditor of *Action Sports Hockey*, as well as being the New York correspondent for the *Toronto Star*. His articles have appeared in *The New York Times, Weekend* magazine, *Sports Illustrated*, and other national publications. Stan and his wife Shirley are coauthors of *Fischlers' Hockey Encyclopedia*.